S0-BKO-942

AGUAYO EXPEDITION INTO TEXAS 1721

AGUAYO EXPEDITION INTO TEXAS / 1721

AN ANNOTATED TRANSLATION OF THE FIVE VERSIONS OF THE DIARY KEPT BY BR. JUAN ANTONIO DE LA PEÑA

BY RICHARD G. SANTOS

JENKINS PUBLISHING CO.
AUSTIN, TEXAS/1981

Jenkins Book Publishing Co.
Austin, Texas
ISBN 0-8363-0149-8

Design by
Larry Smitherman

ACKNOWLEDGMENTS

I wish to extend a sincere and hearty thanks to the following friends and colleagues for their assistance and invaluable cooperation in helping me acquire the various versions of the Peñá Diary: Roberto and Sofia Heredia of Mexico City; Dr. J. Ignacio Rubio Mañe, director of the Mexican National Archives; Dr. Ernesto de la Torre Villar, director of the Mexican National Library; and Dr. Chester Kielman, archivist, University of Texas at Austin.

I also wish to thank Dr. John H. Jenkins for his patience and understanding. Three years is a long time to wait for a manuscript, but neither he nor I envisioned there being four, possibly five, different versions of the Penã diary. No author could ask more from his publisher than patience and understanding, and that I received from Johnny.

Richard G. Santos

FOREWORD

The importance of the Aguayo Expedition to Texas, 1719-1722, which eradicated French hopes to claim Texas and indelibly stamped Spanish influence and culture into the Texas heritage, demands not only a first-rate historian, but one with many special qualifications. In order to accurately portray the Expedition and Texas at this time, the historian must not only be familiar with the writings and history of the period in Mexico, Spain and Colonial Texas, but he must, through long association and study of the period, have a feeling and sympathy for the hardships encountered by the Expedition and of the currents of history working upon Colonial Texas at this time which played such an important factor in determining the successes and failures of the Expedition itself. He must also be capable of reading, comprehending and translating the archaic Spanish used in the various versions of the diary. Such a man is Richard G. Santos of San Antonio.

His scholarship is recognized both in this country and in Mexico, with numerous publications in the fields of history and education carrying his by-line. His articles in various historical journals and mass-media outlets in this country and in Mexico are far too numerous to list. However, among major historical works which have received critical acclaim in both countries are *Santa Anna's Campaign Against Texas* [Waco, 1968], the Mexican Period for *Six Flags of Texas*

[Waco, 1969], and *San Antonio de Bexar, 1 de enero, 1836* [1963, 65, 68]. Major historical articles still being re-printed and circulated include: "From The Inside Looking Around—A Portrait of the Mexican American of Texas," "Documentos Para La Historia de Mexico en los Archivos de San Antonio," and "Provincias Internas—A Brief History of Northern Mexico, Texas and the Southwest."

Santos, who served as Archivist of Bexar County in the Office of the County Clerk from 1963 to 1970, is accredited with transforming the Bexar County Archives into an important historical source through his catalogues, indices and translations of this treasure trove. He is largely responsible for the preservation, filing and retrieval system of these important historical documents dating from 1728 to 1900. This graduate of St. Mary's University became recognized during this period as the leading authority on Colonial Texas History. This work on the Aguayo Expedition cannot fail but to add luster to this reputation.

Santos is a multi-faceted scholar. From 1968 to the present he has specialized in the utilization of history, culture and linguistics in education. During this period he served as Director of the closed circuit television station for the Edgewood Independent School District in San Antonio. In 1971 he began a five year teaching administrative position with Our Lady of the Lake University as Director of Ethnic Studies. That same year he became a part-time instructor in the Graduate School of Urban Studies at Trinity University.

His bilingual education textbooks used in numerous schools throughout Texas and the Southwest include *Tesoros de Mi Raza* (1971), *Raza de Tesoros* (1972), *Escaparate* (1973) *La Rosa Que Nunca Muere* (1972), *El Niño Que Aprendió Solo* (1972), *Tejanitos* (1978), *Vacation Diaries* (1979), *Trip To The Mexican Pyramids* (1980), and *Origin of Spanish Names* (1981). Santos has also published a great number of teachers guides, lesson plans, and has designed, written and produced a number of filmstrips, audio presentations, slide presentations and films. Among the better known documentary films are *Abrazo* (one hour film for KMOL TV, San Antonio, 1976), *Tejanos* (one hour film for KHOU TV, Houston, 197), and his own productions: *Quinceanera - A Celebration of Adulthood* (1978), *Amichel - Tejanos of the Lower Rio Grande* (1979), and *Amichel Revisited* (1981). He has also produced two 45 rpm records and four albums currently used in various school districts with an accompanying *Cancionero-Songbook* (1981).

In the field of history, Santos wrote the introductions for *The Battles of Texas* (Waco, 1968), *The Rangers of Texas* (1969), *Guide to the History of Mexico* (Austin,

1970), *Tejano* (Washington, 1970), and served on the editorial board of *Papers of the Texas Revolution* (Austin 1973). In 1974 he was granted membership in the *Sociedad Nuevoleonesa de Historia, Geografia y Estadistica* of Monterrey, Nuevo León, and the following year he was awarded the Alonso de León medallion for outstanding contribution to the History of Mexico. The award was presented for his unfinished biography of Juan N. Seguin which he translated and published in the *Texas Handbook*, Volume III (1976).

Also in 1976, Santos received his graduate degree in linguistics from Trinity University in San Antonio. His current work schedule includes finishing the biography of Juan N. Seguin, an edited translation of the diary of Jean Louis Berlandier, and further filming and recording of Tejano folklore and culture.

Richard G. Santos brings all these diverse but much needed talents to this edited translation of the diary of the Aguayo Expedition. Each of these talents was needed in order to accomplish a definitive account of this important historical event which shaped the early destiny of Texas.

Tony E. Duty
Waco

CONTENTS

Diary of Don Joseph De Azlor y Virto De Vera 17

The Spanish Presidios of Texas and La Salle's Fort St. Louis 83

Route of the Aguayo Expedition 106
Footnotes 111
Bibliography 133

DON JOSEPH DE AZLOR Y VIRTO DE VERA SECOND MARQUIS DE AGUAYO, AND THE DIARY OF HIS EXPEDITION TO THE LAND OF THE TEXAS 1719-1722

Spanish control of Texas in 1719 was limited to seven missions and two presidios. Six of the missions were in what is now East Texas. They were: San Francisco de los Texas, Purísima Concepción, San Joseph de los Nazonis, Nuestra Señora de Guadalupe, Nuestra Señora de los dolores, and San Miguel de los Adaes. The Presidio de [los] Texas can best be described as a wandering military garrison. The missions also seem to have moved about in their founding and re-establishments by Domingo Terán de los Ríos in 1691, Domingo Ramón in 1716, and Martín de Alarcón in 1718. Native Indian mobility, weather and geography seem to have been the major causes for the site changing.

The seventh mission, San Antonio de Valero, and the second Presidio, San Antonio de Bexar, founded in 1718, were also moved at least three times. In these formative years, the Spaniards were not so concerned with exact locations as they were with general areas. By 1719, the geographic area of concern was "the Province of the Texas Indians."

The French had created this concern by slowly descending down the Mississippi River from New France. As early as 1712, they had begun to look upon Louisiana as a springboard and entrance-way to the mines and cities of northern New Spain. Neglected Spanish Texas, however, was in the way.

Louisiana Governor, Antoine de la Mothe Cadillac, ordered Louís de St. Denis in 1713, to open an overland trade route to New Spain. Starting from Natchitoches, St. Denis crossed Texas and arrived at Presidio San Juan Bautista on the Rio Grande on July 18, 1714. The Frenchman was dispatched to Mexico City by the Spanish commandant Don Diego Ramón. In the meantime, St. Denis had met and fallen in love with the commandant's granddaughter. On his return from Mexico City in 1714, St. Denis married Manuela Sánchez de Ramón. Almost two years later, in 1716, the Frenchman led his brother-in-law, Captain Joseph Domingo Ramón, to East Texas.

The Ramón Expedition composed of approximately 65 men, re-established Spanish claim and control of East Texas. The six missions and one Presidio, however, could neither contain the Indians nor exclude the French. St. Denis, for political and marital reasons, felt the time was right for establishing trade relations. He received support from Mobile for his commercial propositions and returned to Presidio de San Juan Bautista where he arrived on April 19, 1717. He was promptly arrested and dispatched to Mexico City. St. Denis was imprisoned until November 22, when he was released on bail. The Frenchman jumped bail and managed to escape to Natchitoches.

In the meantime, another Spanish expedition to the land of the Texas had been approved. Martín de Alarcón had been appointed Governor of Coahuila and Texas and ordered to help support and colonize the province. His expedition entered Texas in mid-1718, bringing at least 30 families. On the first week of May he established the Presidio and Villa San Antonio de Bexar, and mission San Antonio de Valero. Alarcón then proceeded to east Texas more in a show of force for the benefit of the Indians and the French than anything else.

Alarcón, however, failed to impress anyone. The Indians took the gifts he brought and left. The Franciscan Friars complained that Alarcón had not successfully colonized the province. The Government refused to issue the support, troops, supplies and equipment which he asked for. And the French entrenched themselves at Natchitoches and continued to look hungrily at Texas. The Governor tended his resignation, and it was accepted.

On January 9, 1719, war broke out between Spain and France. Five months later, on May 14, the French surprised and captured the Spanish fortress of Penzacola. Almost a month later the French attacked and captured Mission San Miguel de los Adaes. The Spaniards panicked and retreated to San Antonio, thus abandoning all of East Texas.

Don Joseph de Azlor y Virto de Vera, a wealthy Coahuilan holding the title of Second Marquis de San Miguel de Aguayo, now entered the picture. Born in 1677, Don Joseph came from an illustrious military family in which service to the crown was a tradition, not a duty. He acquired the title of Marquis de San Miguel de Aguayo through marriage. His wife, Ignacia Javiera had inherited the marquisate from her father Don Agustín de Echeverez y Zubiza. Don Agustín had been named Marquis de San Miguel de Aguayo by Charles II on November 23, 1682.

The second Marquis de San Miguel de Aguayo came to Coahuila in 1712 and lived at the historia Hacienda de Patos. In 1716, he donated 200 head of cattle for Ramón's expedition to Texas. Moreover, he supplied and maintained troops at his own expense to protect Coahuila from maurauding Indians. It was not surprising, therefore, that he should volunteer his services as soon as he learned of the French invasion of East Texas.

The Marquis de Valero, Viceroy of New Spain, appointed Don Joseph de Azlor y Virto de Vera Governor and Captain-General of the provinces of Coahuila and Texas. The Marquis de San Miguel de Aguayo apparently took office on December 19, 1719. He immediately began to make preparations for the trip to East Texas. In the meantime, Friar Antonio Margil de Jesús from the College of Nuestra Señora de Guadalupe de Zacatecas, asked and received permission to establish a mission at San Antonio. The mission was formally established on February 23, 1720, and named San Joseph y San Miguel de Aguayo.

By June 23, 1720, all was ready for the expedition to Texas. A drought and unexpected loss of horses, mules and cattle delayed the departure until November 15. On that day the expedition formally set out from Monclova, Coahuila and did not return until May 31, 1722.

When the Marquis assumed the governorship, there were only one mission and one presidio left in Texas. Both were in San Antonio. When he left Texas, there were ten missions, four presidios, and over 300 Spaniards, some with families, settled in Texas. Never again would the French threaten Texas.

The most important eye-witness of the expedition was none other than the chronicler and Chaplain-Major of the Batallion, Franciscan Br. Juan Antonio de la Peña. Nothing is presently known of this extremely important personality other than the fact that he wrote and signed the diary. The diary itself is almost as mysterious as its author. There are at least four, perhaps five, versions of the diary.

The best known version of the diary [referred to as Diary A in the translation] was that published in 1722, by Juan Francisco de Ortega Bonilla in Mexico City. Another version [Diary B] is on file in the Mexican National Archives in RAMO DE HISTORIA, TOMO 28, EXPIDIENTE #1, ff. 3r through 62v. A third version [Copy C] is on file in Spain and that version was compared with the published [1722] version, corrected, and then printed in *DOCUMENTOS PARA LA HISTORIA ECCLESIÁSTICA Y CIVIL DE LA PROVINCIA DE TEXAS* [Madrid, 1961]. A fourth version [Diary D] is on file in the Mexican National Archives in MANUSCRITOS DE LOS CONVENTOS, Legajo 94, Expidiente #2. A possible fifth version [Diary E] is said to be a handwritten copy of the published 1722 version and is on file in the Mexican National Archives in RAMO DE HISTORIA, TOMO 302, EXPEDIENTE #6, ff. 1r through 52v.)

It is imperative to note that there are numerous differences among the versions of the diary. Yet each and every version claims to be the "true, accurate and correct copy." We do know for sure, however, that the famous and frequently used printed copy is not the original. It could not be. It is a *printed* version and based on the manuscript actually hand-written by de la Peña.

It is very possible that none of these four or five versions are actually the original and that all of them are based on an original. It is possible that the original was dictated at various times and that mistakes were made in writing the dictation. It is also possible that the original manuscript was hand delivered to the printer in 1722, and that it no longer exists.

With all this in mind we proceed to the following translation of the Peña diary based on five versions of the original manuscript.

If I were as secure in carrying out orders as I am happy to receive them, I could well assure myself of the accuracy which I desire to merit the honor bestowed upon me by the Marquis de San Miguel de Aguayo in ordering me to write this diary as a faithful eye-witness of the accomplishments of this glorious enterprise. I have achieved my greatest honor in being chosen by *His Lordship*[1] to go in service of Our Lord, the King [may God protect him], as Chaplain Major of these troops.

I should begin this narration by first stating the motives which prompted this expedition so that it may be known by all for all times. They are reduced [to the fact] that twenty-one years ago, upon the instigation of merchants in Paris, the

French settled Mobile,[2] a port on the Gulf of Mexico [which is] twelve leagues away from our Presidio Santa María de Galve [commonly called Penzacola].[3] Since then they *have*[4] extended themselves some three hundred leagues to the Natchitoches River which they called Rivera Roja bordering Los Adays[5] in the Province of Texas. Their people have extended themselves some four hundred leagues up the coast from the Río de la Empalizada[6] which they call Misuri [sic.].[7]

Taking advantage of the alliance between the two crowns, they surprised the Presidio de Penzacola and at the same time invaded the Province of *the*[8] Texas on the 19th *day*[9] of June of the past year of 1719. Their superior *forces*[10] obliged the Spaniards to abandon [the Province] *retreating*[11] with the missionary fathers of the six missions[12] which they had erected to the Presidio San Antonio de Bexar[13] which is located on the boundary with Coahuila[14] and which is 240 leagues from Los Adays, [eastern] boundary of Texas.

[In light] of this information, His Excellency [the Viceroy] ordered that the largest *company*[15] possible from the Kingdom of [New] León,[16] town of Saltillo[17] and Parras[18] were to be raised with *utmost*[19] urgency for the relief of the Province. The Marquis de San Miguel de Aguayo was encharged the task of equipping and supplying [the company]; as it was done. Eighty-four men from the three districts of the town of Saltillo were recruited from the fifth day of September until the twenty-eighth day when they left and were furnished by His Lordship with clothing, arms, horses, and provisions for a year. [The provisions consisted] of flour, maize and cattle amounting to over nine thousand pesos above the twelve thousand committed for this purpose by His Excellency [the Viceroy].

As soon as the Marquis received news of the invasion, he wrote His Excellency offering his estate, life, and arms in service of Our Lord the King [may God protect Him]. In his reply, His Excellency sent the dispatches confirming upon him [the Marquis], in the name of His Majesty, the governorship of these provinces. Upon receiving it, [the Marquis] stated that even if he had gone as an armed foot soldier, he would have done so happily in service of His Majesty in this glorious enterprise because since the discovery of America there had never been a more valiant enemy. And, because it was of the utmost importance to secure these dominions from such an immediate danger which threatened them. He set out immediately and arrived at this [town of Monclova] de Coahuila[20] on the twenty-first of October. Upon being informed of the state of things, he reported to His Excellency on the few forces that existed on the frontier and their exposure due to the openness of the terrain. The same was also true of these kingdoms.

On the basis of this report His Excellency ordered the recruitment of five hundred men from the districts of the cities of Querétaro, Zacatecas, San Luís Potosí, Celaya, and the town of Aguas Caliente. He also ordered the Marquis to be encharged with one year's salary [for the troops] on the basis of 450 pesos per soldier plus twenty-five thousand pesos more from the [treasury of the secretariat] of War and Peace.

In the meantime, the Catholic zeal of Our Lord the King [may God protect him] was so *excited*[21] with the *matters*[22] concerning our Holy Faith, which was the mean of *founding*[23] missions, [that he ordered] the *establishment*[24] of San *José*[25] y San Miguel de Aguayo, with three nations of numerous Indians, one league from the Presidio de San Antonio under which protection its permanency was assured. It was approved by His Excellency who then ordered the regular assistance be given its founding.

By[26] the first of April of the present year of 1720, the five hundred men began to leave their said districts already equipped and provisioned for the journey by the representative of the Marquis. They bought *3,600*[27] horses for their transportation and expedition which from its first steps was very difficult for it being during the driest season. They arrived at [Monclova de] Coahuila on the 23rd of June with only 560 horses. The rest had died or had been *left*[28] incapacitated enroute. Along with this set-back, the 560 horses which did arrive were not able to continue the march due to extreme fatigue. Thus, it was necessary for the soldiers to stop at [Monclova de] Coahuila and send out for new mounts to all the pastures where there were horses. Three thousand four hundred [horses] were thus gathered, but they did not arrive at [Monclova de] Coahuila until the latter part of September due to the continuation of the most rigorous drought which had ever been experienced during the whole summer.

The mule packs which had left Mexico City on the twenty-fourth of April carrying the clothing, arms, powder and six artillery pieces, all of which had been acquired through orders of His Lordship, did not arrive until mid-October.

With the news that all which was being awaited was beginning to *arrive,*[29] the Marquis formed a batallion of mounted infantry with the name of San Miguel de Aragón. He divided the five hundred men into eight companies, and with the power vested upon him by the Viceroy to name officers, he selected Don Fernando Pérez de Almazán as his Lieutenant Governor and Captain General.[30] He also gave titles of captaincy to Don Thomas de Zubiria,[31] Don Miguel Colón,[32] Don *Manuel* Gabriel Costales,[33] Don Manuel Herrera,[34] Don Francisco Bezerra Luque,[35] Don

Jose Arroyo,[36] Don Pedro de Uribe,[37] and Don Juan Cantú.[38] He also named all the junior officers.

The mail from Mexico City arrived on the fifth of October. In the dispatches His Excellency gave new instructions to the Marquis to enter and recover, for the Dominion of His Majesty, the Province of the New Phillipines. [Moreover], in light of the news which His Excellency had just received from a messenger ship concerning the cessation of hostilities between the two Crowns, His Lordship, after re-establishing the missions, was to wage only defensive war in case the French encroached upon His Majesty's arms. His Excellency also sent His Lordship instructions, quoting dispatches which His Excellency had received from Our Lord the King [may God protect him]. In them, His Majesty explains the manner with which the French *are to be dealt with*[39] and that His Lordship is to ask for and admit any Frenchman wishing to serve in his Royal Armies, or wishing to come and reside with the Spaniards. Even though [His Lordship] did not explain his immediate reaction to the orders, which limited his desires to attempt to completely secure these parts, he did say that even this much more would be sacrifice to blind obedience.

Because clothing had not come ready made, all the time since the arrival of the mule droves was used to complete the clothing. It was not until the fifteenth of November that his Lordship ordered the battalion to March. Before doing so, he ordered the benediction of the standards in a solemn ceremony to Our Lady of Pilar who was to be carried in our lead standard together with San Miguel and San Rafael with PUGNATE PRO FIDE ET REGE[40] as its motto. On another standard there appeared Our Lady of Guadalupe with San Miguel and San Francisco Xavier. Our Father and *Patrón* Santiago[41] appeared on the third standard.

The artillery and the rest of the companies were given the first and best exercise in firing their arms with the repeated salvos which they fired during the ceremony. [The ceremony] included a *procession, mass,* and *sermon.*[42] The Governor enlightened the day by serving brandy to the troops and by hosting a splendid banquet for all the *officers*[43] and missionary fathers of the province.

The Marquis had to issue various instructions for the governance of the Province as well as for the conveyance of the provisions from Saltillo and Parras which are 400 leagues from the boundary of Texas. Five hundred mules were needed to convey the said provisions. This did not include those [mules] already sent ahead to San Antonio with a great deal of provisions. Additionally, there were 400 mules marching along with the battalion which [the Marquis] placed under the command of Lieutenant *General*[44] Don Fernando Pérez de Almazán.

The march began on the *16th*[45] of November, led by a picket of veteran soldiers knowledgeable of the terrain. They were followed by the companies in order of seniority, each covering their own herds of horses and equipment. They in turn were followed by the mule herds carrying the food and war supplies. Thence came the herds of cattle and sheep. The entire line was covered by a captain and his company.

Because the terrain is known as far as the Rio Grande, this leg of the march was not included in the diary. From the onset, the march encountered difficulty. A lagoon had formed on the Camino Real, and the necessary detour took three days.

On the 25th the expedition arrived at the Rio Sabinas which is 25 leagues from [Monclova de] Coahuila. [The river] had been over-flowing for quite some time due to the autumn rains which were as fierce as the summer drought. Finding the river impassable, the Lieutenant General ordered the construction of a canoe because the *flood*[46] had carried away the two which had been ordered made beforehand by the Marquis. The water receded in the meantime and advantage was taken of a long stretch of rocks which crossed the river. [The river] was crossed with much difficulty due to the rapid current. One of the first soldiers to attempt the crossing was drowned. Captain Don Miguel Colón and some other soldiers were also under much peril when they fell into the river. *Three weeks were spent in the delay*[47] of crossing the companies, equipment, droves, and cattle.

By December 15th the crossing of the Rio Sabinas was completed. The 25 league distance to the Rio del Norte, vulgarly called the Rio Grande, was covered by the 20th of December on which date the battalion arrived and camped upon its bank. The river was so rich in water that it was more than musket shot in width and a rod and a half in depth. Informed by the natives that it would take a long time for the waters to recede, the Lieutenant General ordered the construction of wooden rafts. After three [rafts] were constructed, the crossing was able to begin after Christmas.

At the same time, the Marquis arrived at the Rio del Norte from [Monclova de] Coahuila. Arriving with him was the Very Reverend Priest, Friar Isidro Felix de Espinosa,[48] President of the missions of Texas of the College of the Holy Cross of Querétaro. A few days later [there arrived] Doctor Don Joseph Codallos y Rabal,[49] Commissioner and Qualifier of the Holy Office [of the Inquisition], Synodal Examiner of the Bishop of Guadalajara and ex-visitor of the Ecclesiastical Judge of Mazapíl and of Saltillo. He was entering Texas with the title of Vicar General with all powers *delegated*[50] upon him by the Bishop of Guadalajara to whose jurisdiction the Province belongs.[51]

His Lordship went to visit missions San Bernardino[52] and Santiago del Valle de la Candela[53] which are off the Camino Real. *On his own*[54] he clothed all the Indians of all ages as he had previously done at missions San Miguel de Aguayo[55] and San Buenaventura[56] in the vicinity of [Monclova de] Coahuila.

Although with great difficulty, the river crossing was continued by using different types of rafts. One [such raft] was made of cowhide. It did not work effectively due to lack of tar. With *various*[57] experiments, only one raft which had ten barrels underneath worked out. Even though no more than two, *I mean six*[58] loads could be crossed at one time, the harsh weather of frost, snow and rain caused further delay. The crossing could best be carried out on rainy days because the cold would subside.

Fifty Nadador[59] Indians were constantly in the water guiding the rafts. They worked with so much devotion that all except four of them became ill. They were warmed and encouraged by the example of the Marquis who was assisting on the river bank. He also gave them supplies of brandy, chocolates and an abundance of food in return for all the work they did.

On the second day of February His Lordship received an express dispatch from San Antonio carrying letters from the captain of that Presidio, Don Mathías García. He reported in the letters that he had just been informed by some Indians of the *Sana*[60] Nation that Captain Luís de San Denis[61] and some other Frenchmen had convened all the Indian Nations. The convocation was some 30 leagues from the said Presidio, but he [Captain Mathías García] did not know its purpose.

This information was brought before a Council of War by His Lordship. It was decided in the Council to dispatch a detachment of 100 men from all the companies with all haste. Sixteen other veteran soldiers, all Presidial troops and knowledgeable in the terrain, were also sent to protect San Antonio and, if necessary, to sally forth and contain the enemy. The detachment left after being divided into two companies. The companies were led by the first captains Don Thomas Zubiria and Don Miguel Colón. The commander [of the detachment] was Lieutenant General Don Fernando Pérez de Almazán.

When [the Lieutenant General] arrived at San Antonio, he learned that in the meantime Captain García had dispatched some very confidential Indians to explore the area under captain Juan Rodríguez who is one of the chiefs of the

Ranchería Grande. The chief had gone to San Antonio with fifty families to ask for a mission. He returned [to San Antonio] on the 25th of February saying he had gone as far as the vicinity of the Brazos de Dios River and had not been able to find the Indians of the Ranchería Grande who lived a lot closer. He presumed that the Ranchería had gone to the convocation. He added he did not dare go any further. Upon returning to San Antonio, he was told by his Indians that a Sana Indian had been there looking for him. [The Sana Indian] wanted to tell him that the Indians of the Ranchería Grande and many other [Indian] Nations were at the meeting with the French. The Indians were armed with many muskets, had many horses, and were located between the two branches of the Brazos de Dios River above the Texas Road.

In light of this information, the Lieutenant General decided to send a party of 30 men from the batallion and from the veteran soldiers under the command of Captain Don Mathías García. They went as far as the Brazos de Dios River which is some 80 leagues distant from San Antonio. They returned because they were not able to cross a very large lagoon which had been formed by the flood between the two branches of the Brazos de Dios River. From this point he was able to see some smoke on the other side [of the lagoon]. The convocation was being held there. They did not encounter any Indians either going or coming.

The Marquis *received*[62] this information two days before the crossing of the Rio [Grande] was effected. On this day and the following day His Lordship distributed and dressed 60 Indians who had helped with the crossing of the rafts and cattle. His Lordship also gave them meat and maize during the whole duration of the crossing.

24th[63]

Everything was crossed on the 23rd of March. On Monday March 24, His Lordship began the march from this side of the Rio Grande with the eight companies less the detachment which was already at San Antonio. Each company had 350 horses, 600 head of cattle, 800 head of sheep, 500 loads of food and war provisions and clothing which were sent ahead. Six hundred loads of clothing, provisions and equipment traveled with His Lordship.

Captains Don Alonso de Cárdenas[64] and Don Juan Cortinas[65] also left with the soldiers which they had in their two companies. They were joined in the march by the President Father, Friar Isidro Felix de Espinosa and by Father, Friar Benito

Sánchez,[66] a Texas missionary who had been at Mission San Juan Bautista[67] at the Presidio del Rio Grande del Norte.[68]

Because from this point forth the road is not so well known,[69] and because part of the road will be over a new route to San Antonio, this account will therefore assume the form of a diary. The direction of the march was straight north.

After about two leagues we passed the site called the *Real*[70] del Cuervo[71] where there is water in small pools most of the year and very good pastures. We arrived at the site called Rosas de San Juan[72] where the march was concluded after five leagues. There was nothing outstanding along the march to report. Most of the route was of glens and creeks which were not very deep. Even though there are some plains with good pastures, the rest are full of bushy thickets which are called mesquite in this area.

5 leagues

25th

On Tuesday the twenty-fifth we had to halt the march so that the troops would not be without mass on such a solemn day. On the twenty-sixth His Lordship also found it necessary not to march due to the loss of many horses and loads. They were recovered.

27th

On Thursday the twenty-seventh His Lordship departed from the campsite on the Rosas de San Juan. Due to the density of the fog with which the day had dawned, a soldier from the herd of horses was lost. His Lordship left two soldiers to search for him. We marched straight northeast for about two leagues to where we took a road over clear and level land. We had left the old road which is rugged and full of thickets. We thence marched three leagues towards the East to where we rejoined the old road which runs east-northeast to the site called Springs of San Diego.[73] This site is nine leagues distant from the Rosas de San Juan. It was necessary to make this long trek due to the lack of watering spots between the sites. Another soldier was lost enroute when he chased a run-away horse. His Lordship sent two soldiers to search for him.

9 leagues

28th

On Friday the twenty-eighth we departed on a northeastern course for about half of the journey. Thence, we went towards the east until we made camp at the Caramanchel Creek[74] which is about five leagues distant [from the previous campsite]. At this campsite there is abundant water during autumn and winter. It also has very beautiful pastures. Along the banks of the creek there are many turkeys which are called Guajolotes.[75] All along the route there is an abundance of quail, rabbits, and hares.

5 leagues

29th

On Saturday the twenty-ninth[76] we marched two leagues on an east-northeast course as far as the Nueces River.[77] Its crossing was facilitated by a bridge of trees, branches and dirt. Previously we had crossed a very deep, dry creek[78] with a number of pools where there is water most of the year. From the said Nueces River we took a northeasterly course to the camp of the Tortuga [creek].[79] The march was terminated at this point after traveling five leagues. There is a large water pool at this site with water all year round. [The pool] had many fish. It is surrounded by a large plain with abundant pastures. There are many turkeys, peacocks, quail and hares in its vicinity.

5 leagues

30th

On Sunday the thirtieth we marched in an east-northeasterly course for the whole journey to the place called Encinos del Rio Frio,[80] commonly called Rio de los Muertos.[81] We traveled over very open country covered with various types of fragrant and colorful *flowers.*[82] There are many turkeys and quail in its vicinity. The march was of six leagues distance.

6 leagues

31st

On Monday the thirty-first we left on an east-southeast direction in search of a crossing, a ravine called Rio Frio[83] and which was now carrying water. It is two and a half leagues distant [from the point of beginning]. In its surrounding area there are many trees on one side and many briers and bushes on the other. The detour [for both sides of the Rio Frio] was one league. A soldier got lost in all this, and His Lordship sent out a search party. From this point there are some beautiful meadows all the way to the site called Los Gatos[84] where there are only some small waterholes with little water. It was necessary to divide the horses and mules and send them to different waterholes about a league and a half distant. There were deer, turkeys, quail, and rabbits along the route. The march was of six leagues.

6 leagues

1st
On the first day of April we departed towards the east-northeast for two and a half leagues until we reached a dry ravine.[85] Half a league beyond we reached a deeper one with water which is called Arroyo Hondo.[86] Its crossing was facilitated by having sent ahead some workers to fix the crossing. The road to that point is full of brambles and briers. There are a great number of pecan and other types of trees in the vicinities of the ravine *and creek.*[87] [From the Arroyo Hondo] the land is very level and beautiful. There are many meadows of different kinds of flowers. The day's journey was concluded after seven leagues at the site called Tulillo[88] where there is water in various waterholes all year round. *Two leagues before we had passed the site called Las Cruzes*[89] *where there are many trees and water year round.*[90] Along the entire route of this day's journey there is an abundance of white tail deer, wild sheep, turkeys, rabbits and quail.

7 leagues

2nd
On Wednesday the second day of April, His Lordship delayed the departure due to the fact that the night had been so stormy and rainy that the herd of horses and mules had stampeded. All the horses and mule droves of one company were lost. After having collected everything, we were able to march three leagues to the site which is called Charco de la Pita[91] where there is water all year round. We had marched northeasterly in the rain and for this reason, as well as for the fact that there was no [drinking] water ahead, we halted at this site. The road has some brambles and briers, but the remainder has beautiful meadows with an abundance of turkey and deer.

3 leagues

3rd
On Thursday the third we continued the journey for about three leagues in a straight east-northeasterly direction. For the remainder of the day's journey we headed north-northeast, and northeast. The departure had been delayed because the night before had been very stormy with high winds, rain and thunder all of

which frightened the herds. At dawn all the horses and the mules of two companies were missing. Even though they were not recovered until nine in the morning, we were still able to march for nine leagues to the Rio Medina.[92] The March was difficult but unavoidable because there was no water in between. The Marquis left two veteran soldiers in search of a soldier, who was a new recruit, who had gotten lost gathering the herds. About three leagues of the road is through a forest of different types of trees such as pecan, oaks, and white oaks. There were also some grape vines with fruit already in blossom. One of the vines was so thick that it had a trunk of one *vara* in circumference! The remainder of the road was a plain where there were *very*[93] many deer and white tail deer. At one time there were some 300 or 400 of them in the vicinity of the troops. The soldiers who covered the line chased two deer into the herd of horses and were thus able to capture them. Many more could have thus been captured by the soldiers on horseback had it not been for not wanting to disrupt the march. There were also turkeys and quail in abundance.

9 leagues

4th

On Friday the fourth after bringing in the lost soldiers, High Mass and several Low Masses were celebrated in the morning in honor of Our Lady of Sorrows. We left and entered the Province of the Texas, New Phillipines, which is divided from the Province of Coahuila, New Estremadura, by the Rio Medina.[94] [We marched] east-northeast for about three leagues to the Leon Creek[95] which carries water most year round and always keeps some in pools. We thence declined our direction to the northeast over a beautiful plain all the way to San Antonio. The road from the Rio [Medina] to the Leon Creek travels over low hills and good valleys with numerous flints along the route which can also be found at various places from the Rio Grande to San Antonio. We arrived [at San Antonio] on the same fourth day [of April]. It is six leagues distant from the Rio Medina.

6 leagues

On the same fourth day [of April], feast day of Our Lady of Sorrow, we arrived at the town and garrison of San Antonio de Bexar.[96] There was great jubilation among all of us as well as among those who awaited us to incorporate themselves with this glorious expedition. After having made camp, the Governor and the entire battalion went to Mission San Antonio de Valero which had been dedicated to the Glorious San Antonio de Padua[97] so that the soldiers might offer their hearts to God from these very first steps that they were taking in the Province of the New Phillipines. All of the priests received Our Lord the King [may God protect him] in the person of the Governor with the *Te Deum Laudamus*[98] in accordance with the *Benedictus qui venti in nomine Domini.*[99] Reciting the prayers of the Holy Church, they implored and blessed the progress of His Majesty's arms in the propagation of the Catholic faith. The missionary priests who were waiting here to incorporate themselves into the expedition included the Most Reverend Father Friar Antonio Margil de Jesús, Commissary of the Holy Office [of the Inquisition], founder and former Guardian of the Apostolic Colleges of the Holy Cross of Querétaro and Our Lord Christ of Guatemala, Prefect and current President of the missions of Texas.[100] [Also waiting but] belonging to the Apostolic College of Our Lady of Guadalupe de Zacatecas were: *apostolic preacher Friar Gabriel de Vergara;*[101] *apostolic preacher, Friar Joseph Guerra;*[102] apostolic preacher, friar Joseph Rodríguez;[103] brother, friar Joseph *Albadadejo;*[104] and brother, friar Joseph Pita.[105]

Even though the Governor arrived with the *firm*[106] determination of resuming the march on Holy Saturday, he cancelled the march after being informed that the horses were utterly exhausted due to the rigorous winter they had experienced. [The horses] would not be able to make the long journey if they were not allowed to recuperate. Also, [the expedition] should not fail to celebrate Holy Week at such an opportune site [as San Antonio]. He gave in to the powerful arguments and persuasion of the priests. His *holy zeal*[107] thus recognized the expediency and necessity that his soldiers, as good Christians who were going to establish the Catholic Faith among so many pagans, should cooperate with their example by meeting the precepts of the Church. Moreover, there was the fact that most had not made confession the year before, because at that time some of them had been levied (into service) and others had been on the *field.*[108] To cultivate their souls through the holy mission of the Word of God, *a number of sermons*[109] were preached. The stay at this town was thus prolonged with much satisfaction to all. The priests reaped much fruit from the pulpit as well as through their love and their continuous assistance in the confessionary.

Because in the meantime the troops were not employed in the service of the King, the Governor, for the good of both Provinces ordered several very important things. Since both Provinces lacked salt, he sent a company of 40 soldiers to discover some salt fields reported by the Indians and which were thought to be nearby. Even though they went fifty leagues distant, they were not able to find the main salt field. They then learned from Indians who knew [the salt fields] that they were some 40 leagues further on. They also told them they would not benefit by their discovery because of the distance and because in that vicinity there lived many warring Indian Nations. The [warring] Indians have repeatedly impeded the gathering of salt by 60 or 70 armed men who have come from the New Kingdom of León.[110] Many deaths have occurred on both sides.

Even though 22 days were spent in exploring so much terrain, it was not a total loss. On their return they found two salt fields nearby; one was a quarter day's journey from San Antonio, and the other was to a side of the Camino Real from Rio Grande. Even though [the salt fields] were presently flooded by the year's irregular rain, they were assured by the Indians who lived *there*[111] that during the dry season there is excellent salt as was proven by the sample which they brought and which the Indians said they had gathered last January.

The Governor was also very worried about the lack of news from the 40 man detachment which His Lordship had dispatched from the Rio Grande under the command of Captain Don Joseph Ramón.[112] They had left San Antonio *on the tenth of March*[113] to occupy La Bahía del Espíritu Santo.[114] [His Lordship] sent four trusty Indians on Holy Friday [to La Bahía]. On the 18th of April the Lieutenant and four soldiers sent by Captain Don Joseph Ramón arrived at San Antonio. They brought the happy news that they had taken possession of La Bahía in the name of Our Lord the King. The Holy Cross and the Royal Standards were unfurled on the feast day of Our Lady of Sorrows.

Thirty-two days were spent on the trip from San Antonio, because the Indian guide had not been able to ascertain the route. Also, there was some delay in crossing the swollen rivers. The lieutenant, however, was able to return to San Antonio in six days, and he figured there were no more than 60 leagues to La Bahía.[115] They say [the bay] is very beautiful, and even though it has not yet been sounded due to the lack of wood in that area to make a canoe with, it should be able to nestle many ships in its bosom.

The news was celebrated with the joy befitting such an important and necessary [discovery] because that [place] shall be the key facilitating the exploration of the Province. By defending that entrance [to Texas], all the necessary assistance can be brought from Vera Cruz in a few days.

On the twenty-sixth of April the Marquis dispatched this information by express to the Viceroy for his knowledge. [He also informed him] that the journey was about to be resumed. At the same time he informed His Excellency that even though the soldiers salary was sufficient, it was not enough to maintain them if they were to be continued to be supplied overland. He added that they were *likely*[116] to run short [of supplies] due to the contingency of the rivers and the 400 leagues distance to Los Adays from Saltillo and Parras from where they are brought. In light of this he asked His Excellency to grant him permission to bring the supplies to La Bahía from Vera Cruz. He pointed out that only His Excellency's license was necessary for the purchase or for the charter of a bilander for that which was presently needed to be brought for the maintenance of the Province. [He added] that in this way an important maritime route would be discovered.

Assuming that His Excellency would give him the necessary permission, His Lordship wrote his agent in Mexico [City] instructing him to buy or charter the bilander. [He also ordered him] to send him as fast as possible the supply of flour, maize and other items for which he asked.

After dispatching the mail, His Lordship spent *the day*[117] visiting Mission San Antonio *de Valero*[118] located next to the Presidio. He spent another day at Mission San Joseph y San Miguel de Aguayo which His Lordship had founded a year before with three Indian Nations which had been congregated. It's about a league and a half downstream from the Presidio. At both missions he distributed clothing to all the Indians. [He also gave them] other articles which they esteem very highly. He dressed about 240 Indians including maidens and children at Mission San Antonio de Valero, and 227 at Mission San Joseph y San Miguel de Aguayo. He thence clothed the fifty Indians, including maidens and children, which had been brought by [Indian] captain Juan Rodríguez of the Ranchería Grande. They had come asking for a mission for themselves and for others of their retinue.

In a Council of War His Lordship proposed, and it was approved by votes, to blaze a new road and to take the said Juan Rodriguez and other Indians as guides. The reasons for this decision were as follows: [first] because His Lordship was well aware of the great difficulties encountered en route by such a large train on the roads which have been used in Texas to date. [Second], because of the lagoons and swollen rivers. [Third], because of the heavy brush in the Great Forest which is thus called because of the many leagues which it runs and because its detour is 25 leagues distant. [Fourth], because the road is not well cleared. [Fifth], because of the reports which His Lordship had been receiving. And finally, because Juan Rodríguez, the Indian, had lately volunteered to guide [His Lordship] over good, open plains where there were many rivers and creeks to cross divided by many tributaries. [It should be noted] that the waters meet further south making the rivers so swollen that their crossing is impractical during the rainy season such as this winter has been. The Great Forest would also be avoided by edging around where it begins.

All during this time various squads made a number of runs, by order of the Marquis, to contain the Indians which were then in the surrounding area. [The reason for this] was that just two days before the arrival of His Lordship to San Antonio, a mule pack left the Presidio and a driver was killed and a soldier injured in a skirmish. His Lordship also ordered these runs because of the possibility that the Indians might be Apaches. The order was given to bring back as many live Indians as possible to gift them [with presents] and to discuss with them the value of an alliance with their Nation which extends all the way to New Mexico.

On the tenth of May His Lordship realized that the horses had recuperated, so he ordered the march to resume on the thirteenth. Because we were about to enter land infested with enemies, he also ordered whatever company was on guard to become the picket company. The equipment, horse herds, mule droves and cattle were to march in their same place in the formation with another Company covering the line.

13th of May

On Tuesday the thirteenth we continued the march towards [the land of the] Texas.[119] We took a northeast course for one league meandering thereafter in a northeasterly direction until we reached the place where the water is drawn for Mission San Antonio.[120] There are so many grape vines there with beautiful clusters of unripe grapes that they seem to have been planted by hand. [The course of the march] thence declined towards the east-northeast for *a league*[121] before returning to the northeast to the Salado Creek[122] where we stopped for the day after traveling four leagues. Because some loaded mules and horses had been lost, His Lordship decided to remain at this site for another day. The terrain is very brushy and has many trees. Yet, it is beautiful to see. All that had gotten lost was recovered.
4 leagues

15th
On Thursday the fifteenth we continued the march over a brushy terrain with thorny mesquite trees which give a fruit eaten by the Indians. There were also many heavy oak trees. All of this left many clear places along the route which is very level. We traveled for *one league*[123] northeast, a quarter east-northeast until we reached some low hills from whence could be seen much level and open land deemed very appropriate to *all*[124] types of cattle. We thence turned towards the north-northeast for about one league, and then two more leagues straight east but varying slightly east-northeast to the Cibolo Creek.[125] There is water here all year round in various pools. The day's journey was for five leagues. We made camp at this site for another day because a soldier and some pack mules had gotten lost. All was recovered the same day.

5 leagues

17th
On Saturday the seventeenth we proceeded through a heavy [cluster] of mesquites, oaks and other types of trees, yet the whole route was passable. [We traveled] towards the north for one league and thence one and a half leagues towards the *north-northeast*[126] to a little forest appropriately called Loma de las Flores for at this time there were no plants without flowers in bloom. Because of their beauty as well as for their variety, and because they are so close to one another so that there are no weeds between them, they thus resemble a bouquet or an arrangement in a vase which someone put there. The flowers are as beautiful and fragrant *as garden flowers.* [*Moreover*], *they are found in so many meadows along the route*[127] that they resemble carpets. The land from there is pleasant, level, wide and beautiful in all four directions. From there we traveled northeast a quarter east-northeast over some plains for about two leagues and thence over some low hills. The terrain in this area is full of brambles and briers of mesquite until it comes to a creek which does not have a name. The Governor then named it San Pascual de Baylon[128] because we crossed it on his feast day. Even though [the creek] is not very deep, it does have water all year round. In its vicinity there are sabines, pecans, poplars, mulberry trees and many vines. A quarter league from there the woods start anew all the way to the Guadalupe River.[129] At this time the river is at its *lowest.*[130] It carries a *vara* of water which is so crystalline that the rocks [on the bottom] are visible. Its banks are very wide. The river is born out of three copious springs no more than a quarter league from the crossing. Along the meandering route [of the

river] there is a beautiful forest of different types of trees whose density does not allow the sunlight to enter. A variety of sonorous fowls cry out [from the forest]. [There are also] very many vines which intertwine with the towering trees in an artistic fashion. The water is known to be salutary, for at its springs His Lordship found common ceterach and maiden's hair.[131] Even though there are no places from whence to draw water, they probably exist further down stream. [The area] could well be settled, for the plains are *very*[132] beautiful, and the land must surely be very fertile. Even at this time when many parts of the kingdom are experiencing the dry season of drought and the land is arid and dry, this land remains fertile.

From this site we marched in the same direction [previously given] for about three-quarters of a league to the San Ybon River.[133] [This river] has a deep bed, and it is presently as full as the Guadalupe. Its crest rises so high, however, that it is impassable most of the year depending on the rains and the weather. Because the river comes down from some hills to the north, its origin has not yet been discovered. Its banks are covered with the same types of trees as those of the Guadalupe River. His Lordship ordered a halt on the other side of the river after having marched eight leagues for the day. At all these stops, like asps in the flowers, we found chiggers which annoyed us more than the mosquitos. [There were also] *many*[134] ticks and snakes.

8 leagues

18th

On Sunday the eighteenth we left following a northeast one quarter east-northeasterly course with some variance to the northeast until we reached the site called Peñuelas.[135] This creek keeps water in pools all year round. The rest of the journey was over a level land *with mesquite*[136] off the side of the road. About a league distant to the north begins the great hill country where the Apaches live. The land is known as being very rugged. We made camp that night after having marched four leagues.

4 leagues

19th

On Monday the nineteenth The Governor continued the march on the same course as the day before. [We traveled] over level land for about two leagues. Mesquite and oak trees were found at intervals until we entered a *very*[137] dense area of the same types of trees found at the Guadalupe River. It had been necessary to send ahead workers the day before to clear a way through the trees because the loads could not traverse it. [This forest] extended to the Rio de los Innocentes[138] which was as swollen as the Guadalupe. The river is two and a half leagues from Las Peñuelas. The forest is not so dense on the opposite side. *Both*[139] banks are as pleasant [as Las Peñuelas], and its shade is so dense that it does not allow sunlight to filter through. [From this point] we declined our direction to the northeast a quarter east-northeast for one league. For another league we headed north over level land with a few trees in different places all along the way to the San Rafael Creek.

Without having to ask Tobias,[140] we learned that the fish [at San Rafael] are very good and *very*[141] abundant, as is the case with all the other rivers which we have crossed to this date since leaving San Antonio. Deer and pheasant *are the most abundant*[142] game. There are few rabbits and quail.

We met a squad of Sana Indians who came out to *renew their pledges*[143] of obedience to Our Lord the King [may God protect him]. They were wearing the clothes given them by His Lordship in San Antonio. They were waiting at the said San Rafael Creek.

[The San Rafael] has sufficient trees along its banks and running water most year round. The water, however, is kept in large pools. We camped at this said creek after a day's journey of five leagues.[144]

From this site a party was sent out in search of a soldier who had gotten lost the day before when His Lordship had *sent out*[145] another squad because he had discovered tracks of Spanish cattle. [His Lordship] had wanted to add a treat to the daily rations of the battalion, but it was *not*[146] possible due to the loss of the soldier.

5 leagues

20th

On Tuesday the twentieth we continued the march straight *north-northeast*[147] for a quarter league to a spring called San Isidro which is surrounded by trees. The *rest*[148] of the route was over *very*[149] open terrain with low hills and beautiful valleys. There is a great deal more deer and turkey in abundance, and many were captured without interrupting the march. The day's journey was of six leagues to a small creek. Because it did not have a name, the Governor named it San Bernardino.[150]

6 leagues

21st
On Wednesday the twenty-first we continued the journey in the same direction even though there were signs that the day would be stormy, as it turned out to be. Lightning, thunder and rain began just a quarter league after we started. The storm continued so strongly that the horses got spooked and were running out of line. It was no small task to settle them down. It was impossible to do the same for the cattle. They were so scared that there was no way of moving them forward. It was also impossible to move many loads which were then left behind under the good protection of the company which was covering the march. Because the rain continued for a half a day, camp was made along the banks of the river called Las Carrapatas.[151] We were not able to travel more than one league on this day. We did, however, pass five deep glens, all carrying rain water. The rest of the terrain was open and level.

1 league

22nd
On Thursday the twenty-second because it was the Day of the Ascension, it was celebrated with a sermon and six Masses. For this reason and also because it was decided to await the cattle and mule droves, we stayed at this campsite. Even though there had been some loss [of animals], they rejoined us all that day without difficulty. In the afternoon the party which had been dispatched from the San Rafael Creek to go in search of the lost soldier brought him in, much to the joy of all, because he had fallen into the hands of pagan Indians. He had taken advantage of the supplies and tobacco which His Lordship had given the soldiers by distributing it among the Indians.

23
On Friday the twenty-third the march was continued in a northeasterly course after crossing the Garrapatas River by a belt of rocks which traverses it entirely. [The rocks] make a beautiful fall which exists all year round.[152] The day before the river had risen so much with the storm that it had been impassable. The entire route to the forest of the San Marcos River[153] had low hills and open terrain. *Both*[154] sides of the river abound with a great variety of trees. They also have grape vines. The river carries twice as much water as the previous ones, and its banks are very wide. For this reason it was necessary to lighten the loads. Because we had spent most of the day passing the cattle, we were forced to make camp three quarters league beyond the river at a small creek.[155]

This was a good camp with the shade of many mulberry and blackberry trees which grow twice as large as those of Spain. Also, after having found buffalo tracks, a party was dispatched [after them]. They were able to kill a large one.

The first Spaniards called the buffalo "The Mexican Bull." It is monstrous. *It is like the crow of the hoofed mammals.*[156] Its back is humped like the camel's. Its flanks are lean. Its tail, with the exception of the tip, is short and hairless like the pig's. Its wool covers the entire skin and is dark and heavy but not as fine as the bear's. It has a beard like a goat. Its forehead and neck are adorned with a mane of half a *vara* in length like that of the lion's, and it almost covers its big, black eyes. It has hoofed feet, and it walks like a bull although its appearance is more ferocious for being more powerful and swifter. Its meat is as savory as the best beef.

After having marched three leagues [for the day], we recorded our position at 30 degrees.[157]

3 leagues

24th
On Saturday the twenty-fourth we left traveling over beautiful level land with some intermediate low hills. Everything was covered with beautiful pastures and a variety of flowers all the way to a *deep*[158] creek bordered with trees and branches all entwined. Going down and up its banks was difficult. Because it did not have a name, it was named Santa Quiteria whose feast day was the day before. Also, because its passage was difficult, and especially because there was no campsite ahead, we terminated the day's journey at a creek after traveling four leagues. Since it did not have a name, it was named San Francisco[159] because his feast day was the following day. Since we arrived early [in the day], a detachment of *fifty*[160] soldiers was sent out in search of buffalo. [This number was dispatched] because we were near the hill country where the warring Apache Nation lives. [The soldiers were instructed] to make peace with the Indians if they met any.

4 leagues

25th
The detachment returned on the morning of Sunday the twenty-fifth with three buffalo. They had to make camp the night before because they had gone more than six leagues in search of the [wild] cattle which are very fast. On their return at night they were overcome by a storm with a great deal of thunder, lightning and a

heavy rain. The storm had been so strong that we were not able to march on this day.

26th
On Monday the twenty-sixth after having loaded *most*[161] of the equipment and supplies and after giving the order to mount, it began to rain. The march order was delayed to see if the rain would slacken, but it became so stormy instead that the order to dismount was given. The supplies had to be covered without delay. Had we not done so, we would have run the risk of losing much flour. Even the maize was endangered because once it gets wet it becomes warm and swollen, and it is impossible to dry it out. It would not have been easy [to dry it out] while on the march. This had already occurred with over 500 bushels of maize which the Governor had bought at the Rio Grande. Because the rains had been so strong yesterday and today, several stores and a great deal of the clothes got wet.

27th
On Tuesday the twenty-seventh we left on a northeasterly course all the way to a creek called *Las Animas*[162] which is two leagues distant. The route was over low rolling hills without bushes or trees to the said creek which has many brambles and briers on both sides. A quarter league further on we crossed another small creek[163] with its own trees. The creek showed signs of having its spring nearby. From this point we declined our direction towards the northeast all the way to the *San Xavier River*[164] where we halted. Half a league back we had crossed another big creek[165] with its own forest. The [forest along the] San Xavier is much larger. Both have the same types of trees and vines as those before. Even though this creek is not very wide, it does carry about half a *vara* of water. We killed three buffalo in its environs. The day's journey was of five leagues.

5 leagues

28th
On Wednesday the twenty-eighth we crossed the river at two equal branches. About a musket shot distance away there is a very large pool of water. It took a great deal of time [to go from one branch of the river to the other] because of the heavy brush between them. It was no easy task to pass the cattle and mule droves. For this reason we only traveled four leagues, halting at a creek near the San Xavier. Because it did not have a name, the Governor named it San Ignacio.[166] After crossing the river, the route had been over low and high hills *with many*

obstacles. We also passed another creek[167] with *many* trees along its banks. We had left [camp] in a northeasterly direction for one league, and thence declined towards the north-northeast.

4 leagues

29th

On Thursday the twenty-ninth we stayed at that campsite because the afternoon before we had found buffalo tracks. They were needed to supply the troops, and it was accomplished. Twelve [buffalo] cows were encircled, but not all were killed because they were found in different parts of the campsite.

30th

On Friday the thirtieth we left in a north-northeasterly[168] course with some variance to the north along the march for that day for a distance of five leagues. We reached a creek[169] of abundant fresh water surrounded by trees. It was named San Fernando. We had now crossed twenty creeks.[170]

5 leagues

31st

On Saturday the thirty-first we continued the march in the same direction of north-northeast for about two leagues, thence for about another two leagues to the northeast. About a league and a half distance from the San Fernando we had crossed a creek[171] with plenty of water and many trees. The rest of the road had been over level land with low hills all dressed in a variety of flowers all the way to a mesquite thicket with a clearing [in between] of about one league. The day's journey had been of four leagues to where the halt was made for having reached a river[172] which was impassable at that point. Because we arrived on the eve of Pentecost, it was named Espíritu Santo. Much to the surprise of all, signs of the coming of the Holy Spirit were given not in words but in flames and thunder. A bolt of lightning fell in the camp leaving two soldiers unconscious. One of them regained consciousness immediately; the other took more than an hour. The hat of the latter soldier was riddled as if by a drill. [The bolt] also cracked the flagpole where the soldier had been with his wife and two children.[173] There was no other damage.

As it was later discovered, this is the first branch of the river called Los Brazos de Dios along the other road which used to be taken before to [the land of the] Texas. Between this crossing and the old road, however, the San Xavier River,

Las Animas Creek and all the other creeks which we have passed, come together. Thus, the other crossing[174] is impassable most year round. Due to the continuing rains of autumn and winter, it would have been impassable and inaccessible at this time by so large a train. The big thicket, which the Indians know well and which they can detour around, would have taken 18 or 20 leagues.

4 leagues

1st of June
On Sunday the first and for the other *three*[175] days of the feast of the Holy Spirit we stayed at this campsite. We stayed not only because the river was swollen, but also because the Governor had held a Council of War in which it was decided to dispatch a party of soldiers to reconnoiter the land in search of the Ranchería Grande and learn the designs of the French. We did not know what they were attempting to do with all the [Indian] Nations they had gathered in the vicinity of this river. The course of the river was reconnoitered in the meantime. After having discovered that the river branched out in three tributaries about two leagues upstream,[176] the order to march was given for the day after Pentecost.

4th
On Wednesday the fourth we left in a northeasterly course until we passed the first tributary[177] where there was good pasture. The same was true of the second [tributary][178] which was *very*[179] much more swollen. For having spent so much time crossing the cattle and loads, we halted after only two leagues of travel. We had also received news that the third [tributary][180] was swollen. It was also necessary to clear a path through the thicket [before reaching the third tributary].

2 leagues

5th
On Thursday the fifth we stayed at the same campsite because *the night before*[181] the third tributary had flooded.

6th
On Friday the sixth we departed declining [our direction] towards the *north-northeast*[182] to the third [tributary] of the Brazos which is about one league [distant]. In between there is a deep creek[183] with good pasture. Ever since the previous day's journey, the land had been broken, hilly, and with lots of thicket. This was especially true near the creeks. Because the passage of the third tributary was difficult,

it was not until mid-afternoon that the train was able to cross it. The crossing was a bad one. Several soldiers and mule packs slipped and fell in the rocks and holes.

After turning north, we were forced to make camp three quarters of a league from [the crossing]. The day's journey was of about two leagues. We camped at an excellent site next to a creek which was named San Norberto because it was his feast day and also because it did not have a name.[184]

2 leagues

It was decided to spend the next seven days at this campsite. The corporal of the party which went in search of the Indians had been told that they would be awaited here if they were delayed. As it was, they did not return until the following Thursday. Their trip had been fruitless because they did not meet any Indians in the 30 + leagues which they covered. All they found were the shacks or barracks made by the Indians which had been unoccupied for a long time. They also encountered swamps and lagoons formed by the vast amount of water carried by the river called Brazos de Dios. Because, as the Indians know, this is the place where the San Xavier River and Las Animas Creek enter the river, and it becomes very large at this point.

During this time there arrived at camp 28 mules with supplies and other necessary items. On Friday, the march was suspended so that the meat could be dried. The entire battalion had been supplied [with meat] due to the many buffalo which had been found nearby. The rains, however, did not allow the completion of all the work.

14th

On Saturday the fourteenth we traveled *north-northeast*[185] over open hills and plains which allowed us to see in all directions. The hills were separated by some creeks[186] with deep water crossings. After two leagues we declined our direction towards the northeast until we passed a creek whose trees could be seen from a distance. It was named San Antonio de Padua.[187] We made camp at this site thus concluding our day's journey of five leagues.

5 leagues

15th

On Sunday the fifteenth we continued the march in a northerly direction in order to avoid the swamps and creeks which had been previously reported. We traveled over a beautiful plain well covered with grass and flowers. It was enhanced by the buffalo which could be seen nearby. Three of *them*[188] were scared by the battalion, and shortly thereafter they were consumed.

We arrived at a creek whose white shiny banks seemed to be terraces washed by the currents. This and its beautiful shaded trees were an inviting campsite. Nonetheless, we continued the march for another three leagues in a north-northeasterly direction to a beautiful creek which was named San Joseph de los Apaches.[189] It was so named because it is near their land, and also because this saint might be able to draw them into the fold of the Church. Besides being able to kill many buffalo on this day, one of them was also brought tied and alive into the camp.[190] It served as diversion as well as food.

We observed that we were now at thirty-one and a half degrees latitude.[191]

7 leagues

16th

On Monday the sixteenth we continued on a northeasterly direction with some variances to the north-northeast and perhaps some to the north. The route resembles that of [the day] before. After five leagues we entered a forest of thorny trees which are called mesquite. Its fruit is appreciated by the Indians. We arrived at a creek which was named San Joachín y Santa Ana.[192] Its bordering trees were made more pleasant by the day's sweltering temperature. The day's journey of seven leagues was concluded without having experienced any *considerable*[193] mishaps along the way.

7 leagues

17th

On Tuesday the seventeenth, after having loaded all the equipment in readiness for the march, it had to be suspended due to a report that the next river's crest had risen overnight. Taking advantage of this delay, the Governor dispatched a party to investigate some smoke which was thought to be of the Indians. It was discovered by sight inspection that members of the battalion who had previously been given permission to hunt buffalo, had made the fire.

18th

On Wednesday the eighteenth we made camp at the same place because the river was still flooded. We named the river Jesús Nazareno.[194] It is the second main branch of the two called Brazos de Dios. We discovered a third branch half a league away.[195] It has a luxurious and superior forest on its banks.

19th
The river receded on Thursday the nineteenth. After having found a crossing, the horses and mule droves were sent ahead to ford it. It was done without difficulty. The direction [of the march] was towards the north and then east-northeast over a road with *very*[196] delectable *tall*[197] trees and shade. We made halt at a lagoon called Santa María which is a quarter league wide but not very deep.[198] Its water, however, is sweet. Because the day had started with rain, and because of taking time for the crossing [of the river] by the cattle, the day's journey was of two short leagues.

2 leagues

20th
On Friday the twentieth we marched towards the east-northeast over somewhat hilly terrain. In some places the land opened out with pleasant clearings. After making some variances to the east, the march was halted on a wide plain. The water, however, was not very near. It was not known whether there might be another site with water nearby. At this site which His Lordship named San Sylverio Papa,[199] we captured five buffalo. This was the last game killed of that usually hunted by the soldiers. Over one hundred [buffalos] had been killed since we started to encounter them. Both the soldiers and the captains as well showed their skills and abilities in killing many buffalo. The Governor [himself] killed three on four outings. There was never any injury to the men and only one horse killed and two wounded, and they recuperated. The day's journey was of three leagues.

3 leagues

21st
On Saturday the twenty-first we departed in the direction of *east-southeast*[200] for about a league and then towards the southeast over terrain with mesquite, many oaks, sandy spots, some dry creeks and ravines. We crossed a creek with running water bordered with a pleasant forest. The journey was stopped at a small water pool which was named San Jorge.[201] The day's journey was of five leagues.

5 leagues

22nd
On Sunday the twenty-second we followed the previous direction of southeast with variances towards the lateral winds.[202] We proceeded over land with thickets but not so dense as to create problems. We passed high hills with meadows of a variety of

flowers. After some four leagues we halted at a creek which His Lordship named San Juan de los Jumanes[203] because of the proximity of his feast day.

4 leagues

23rd

On Monday the twenty-third we made camp at the [same] site because there was no report from the scouts. We were also searching for two soldiers who had gotten lost. Other [soldiers] who were going out in search of a campsite found them, and they were very happy to be brought back to the battalion.

24th

On Tuesday the twenty-fourth we continued the march so as not to prolong the journey even though the solemnity of the day demanded that we stay in camp and observe it. We continued in the previous direction over a very difficult forest. Because of its density and because of the uneven terrain, we lost some of the loaded mules. They were found after a thorough search, but even then, two loads were lost.

We continued to a muddy creek, and a short distance thereafter we had to build a bridge to *facilitate*[204] the crossing of a creek with running water which, because of the mud-puddles, was otherwise impassable. The battalion halted at a campsite nearby, even though the site was not very clear. His Lordship named [the campsite] Real de Patrocino de Nuestra Señora.[205] He had marched six leagues.

6 leagues

25th

On Wednesday the twenty-fifth we proceeded in the direction of the southeast and after traversing about three leagues of mesquites we entered a plain which is over one league wide. We then entered a forest of tall trees, and in its thicket we found a creek with running water.[206] Its banks were very steep and cumbersome. This was followed by a forest of oak trees which were very dense in some places. The rest of the seven leagues marched on this day were covered with mesquite and uneven land leading to a fine, narrow clearing next to a small marsh of very warm water. This site was named Angel de la Guarda.[207]

7 leagues

26th

On Thursday the twenty-sixth we marched with some variances towards the east-southeast. After crossing a small creek, we entered a forest with many pecan trees, some oak trees and a diversity of vines with very rich unripe grape clusters. There was also an abundance of plums and green medlars. Half a league distance there was a creek with running water. We traveled southeast downstream another two leagues along both banks. Even though it was narrow, it was open land. All along the creek we observed poplars, willows and many vines. We halted along its banks after traveling three leagues. This campsite was named Nuestra Señora del Camino.[208]

3 leagues

27th

On Friday the twenty-seventh we marched in an east-northeasterly direction and thence to the east for about a league and a quarter over a forest laden with many pecan and oak trees. It was necessary to open a path [through the forest] and level a crossing over two creeks. After crossing them, we encountered a lagoon in a pleasant plain. Thence there was a forest partly covered with oaks. This soon gave way to high, spacious and very pleasant level terrain spotted with oaks. Here we found three old Indian huts.

After having traveled four leagues, we made camp at a creek filled with puddles of rain water. It was named Nuestra Señora de Guía.[209] Here for the first time we were greatly bothered by ticks and chiggers. The animals were pestered by the gadflies.

4 leagues

28th

Saturday the twenty-eighth started with rain and strong winds from the north. This suspended the march for the day. At night we received an express announcing the arrival of a mail carrying ship bringing the happy news of the Majesties' good health. We fired a royal salute. Before [nightfall] we observed our location at this site as being at thirty-two and a half degrees.[210]

29th

On Sunday the twenty-ninth we marched towards the east with some variance to the east-northeast. We traveled four leagues over a clear forest and three muddy creeks to a somewhat brushy clearance where there is an abundance of plum trees. We halted at this campsite which was named San Pedro y San Pablo.[211]

4 leagues

30th
On Monday the thirtieth we camped at the same site because the scouts had not returned from the previous night. Other scouts were dispatched in different directions. They all returned saying the march could continue the next day.

JULY 1st
On Tuesday the first we left in an easterly direction over a small forest of oak trees, sandy terrain, two muddy marshes and two deep creeks with steep and slippery banks.[212] We thence marched towards the southeast along the edge of a marsh. We also had to build a bridge over a small creek. The rest of the terrain had many thickets, and in some places, flint rock. There was also much nettle which [made the march] difficult for the animals because it would make them lame with its poison. Some lame animals were left along the route. We made camp at a small creek with an uncomfortable campsite because it is covered with oak trees. We named it Nuestra Señora de la Estrella.[213]

5 leagues

2nd
On Wednesday the second we marched in the direction of the southeast for one league over tall, scattered trees and then a thicket of very dense oaks. There were also a number of marshes and a creek with running water over which a crossing had to be made. Another muddy creek followed at a short distance. Thereafter there were some marshes which forced us to make detours and search out a high road over the hills. It was in this manner and in the same [southeasterly] direction that we arrived at some old Rancherías next to luxurious and beautiful trees. There was a small creek over which a bridge had to be made. To the right there was a spacious and grassy marsh. We marched six leagues to this site[214] because the scouts had reported we would shortly thereafter encounter level lands and the regular road to [the land of the] Texas. His Lordship decided to continue ahead, and it was done but with much difficulty because the three remaining leagues were made impassable due to the rains of the night before and of that morning. The soldiers could not rely on their horses and were forced to break up the line of march. Those behind had to avoid the tracks of those before them as if they were known precipices because the animals would get stuck in them. Some were forced to manage their horses skillfully because the horses kept running out of strength and wind due to the continuing muck. In order to regroup the battalion, it was

necessary to spend the rest of the day passing some cots and stores which were very few. The rest of the mule packs and equipment was left at various sites along the route. The most advanced cargoes were three leagues behind the battalion's campsite. The day's march was of nine leagues, and the campsite was named by His Lordship Real de la Visitación de Nuestra Señora.[215]

9 leagues

3rd

On Thursday the third His Lordship gave the order to march, for the cargoes were to be further south, over higher ground and on a different direction [from that followed by the batallion]. They found the ground more solid and thus arrived at the said campsite without appreciable damage, for which we were all happy. We had feared some misfortunes with the cargoes if they did not travel over a better route.

4th

On Friday the fourth we spent the day searching for a [passable] bank along the San Buenaventura Creek[216] which was very swollen. A bridge was begun after having found a narrow part. The job was left incomplete for the following day.

5th

On Saturday the fifth His Lordship assigned more people [to the construction of the bridge]. The Governor personally assisted, and the bridge of 24 varas in length and 3 varas in width was completed. The route from one bank of the creek to the other was thus opened, and the road was able to connect with the old road to [the land of the] Texas. The bridge was constructed from tall trees cut from the banks of the creek. Small tree limbs with branches and dirt over them were placed crosswise. The dirt reinforced the fragile and breakable branches.

Two *mountain lion cubs*[217] were found at this site. Their eyes were still closed, and they looked like lions with their colorful furs. They were agreeable to the sight.

6th

On Sunday the sixth we marched in the direction of the northeast, a quarter east-northeast. The first companies began to cross over the bridge when through the negligence of a soldier, a laden horse fell into the water. It was able to get out on the other side, but the cargo was very wet. It was also noticed that the bridge was weakened because one of the props on the right had been thrown out of kilter. It was necessary to use more branches and dirt to patch up the holes which were being discovered. The Governor helped with this task most of the day, and with his assistance everything was passed without risk. We thence proceeded over an open route leaving the *Laguna* de Santa Anna to our right. It is also known as the *[Laguna] de las Cargas*[218] because for eight months in 1719, the cargoes for the relief of the Texas missionaries had been hidden in its forest.[219] We then passed three clearings, two creeks with running water and a clear forest before arriving at another small creek with not too many trees. We halted at this site which His Lordship named Nuestra Señora del Rosario.[220] We had marched four leagues.

4 leagues

7th

On Monday the seventh we marched east, a quarter east-northeast traveling for about two leagues over a road with a light forest of oak trees. The rest of the route was over open, level land. We passed a creek called the Carrizo,[221] and due to its steep embankments the battalions were delayed in crossing it. Several times it was necessary to work on the exit bank because it was very slippery. An easier crossing was sought for the cargoes. After everything was reunited, we made camp at the site called Santa Clara which other people know as Las Cruces.[222] It is thus called because of the many crosses carved on the trees. They were made during the preceding expedition. The day's journey was of eight leagues.

8 leagues

8th

On Tuesday the eighth we continued in the direction of the east-northeast over broken terrain with light forests, hills and clearings. A bridge had to be made on the San Fernando Creek.[223] The battalion then marched to a small creek which His Lordship called Nuestra Señora del Buen Suceso.[224] This creek is on the edge of a spacious plain which is six leagues distant from Santa Clara Creek. Camp was made at this site because of the news that there were Texas Indians nearby. A search was made for their huts.

6 leagues

NOTE:

That morning the Governor had dispatched a party of soldiers on a path which branched off the road towards the south. Reverend President Friar Isidro [Felix de Espinoza] and two other religious went along as guides because they knew the terrain. Three leagues away they found some planted fields cultivated by the Texas [Indians]. After not finding the [Indian] huts, the [soldiers] began to call out in the [Indians'] language. They received a reply from the forest. After crossing a small creek, the [soldiers] met some Indians, most of whom were from the Ranchería Grande. [Indian] captain Juan Rodríguez who accompanied the party [was from the same Nation]. They were received with much pleasure. The party then went to the huts of the said Indians which were a short distance away. They learned that Indians from the Vidays and Agdocas nations were meeting there with those of the Ranchería Grande.

At the same time, the captain of the advance picket found fresh Indian tracks and heard yelling. He halted and sent an ensign with the news to the Governor who was marching at the head of the battalion. His Lordship set out hurriedly with a company, leaving orders for the rest to follow. He ordered [the battalion to] halt at the site where he found the advance picket. His Lordship followed the Indian tracks over a very well used path for about one league distance until he found the party which had been sent out in the morning. The party was with the Indians. At the sound of the trumpet and unfurling of the Royal Standards, the Indians came forth carrying a thin silk flag of white with blue *flurs de lis*[225] which they had gotten from the French. In infantry formation they fired salvos with the muskets that many of them carried. They approached the Governor with signs of submission and reverence. His Lordship ordered them to place their flag below the Royal Standard as a sign of pledging their obedience to Our Lord the King [may God protect him], and also as a sign that His Majesty admitted them under his Royal protection. They were very happy of this.

From horseback His Lordship placed his hands over the heads of men, women and children which is the Indians' sign of pledging obedience. Together there must have been 200 people. After this, His Lordship dismounted at the barrack of an [Indian] captain. He made them understand through an interpreter that he came in peace. They were also told that which was beneficial for them to know of his coming. The said [Indian] encampment which extends for about a league was then toured [by His Lordship]. In the afternoon [His Lordship] awaited the arrival of the Indians who had been out on the hunt. On horseback they came firing salvos together with the other [Indians] until they reached our campsite. The Governor received them with great kindness and sent them away satisfied with some handfuls of tobacco for them to share with their women and children.

9th

The [Indian] captains and a great number of Indians from the Ranchería came to see the Governor on Wednesday the ninth. After continuing to flatter them, [the Governor] gave them beef for their people to eat for breakfast. He also admonished them to keep the peace for they were under the protection of the Spaniards. He asked them to return to where they lived beyond the Brazos de Dios and [promised] to establish a mission [for them] near San Antonio upon his return from the [land of the] Texas. The [Indians] replied that they would do [as requested].

Because the Indians knew that the Trinity River, which was five leagues away, was flooded, His Lordship ordered them to go to the ford which was going to be the river crossing where he would give them clothing and other items. With a bugle call His Lordship ordered the battalion to form a square and [at the same time] asked the [Indians] to be loyal to the Spaniards out of love and fear. The Governor was urged to work his horse in the manner of the Spaniards because of the impression it would make on the Indians, and because they had never seen it before. [His Lordship] worked [the horse] with great skill and schooling through various common turns, and the Indians were aghast.

[His Lordship] placed himself at the head [of the battalion] to continue the march, and the companies followed in sequence. We proceeded in the direction of east-northeast through a light forest of encumbered trees. We found three clearings in a row and passed two muddy creeks where a number of loads fell in. We left [the forest] at the Valle de Linares where the direction was changed to northeast. We found two lagoons and the creek of Santa Rosa[226] which had running water. We also passed some clearings and a forest of pecan and pine trees. We arrived at the Trinity River[227] where we camped amidst the forest [which is] about a musket shot in distance from the river. The day's journey was of five leagues.

5 leagues

10th

On Thursday the tenth the Governor concluded that the river's *flooded state*[228] would continue. Therefore, he ordered the construction of two rafts. One was made by the Indians of the Ranchería Grande. It was made according to their customary method of dry trees and reeds. It was finished in two days, but it was not of much use due to the heavy currents. On the first crossing the Indians became tired and convinced that it could not be used for crossing the river. Meanwhile, the raft made by the soldiers was very large and made of tree trunks and barrels. It was discovered that crossing the river in this raft would be very difficult, and it would take a great deal of time. Moreover, the cargoes of provisions and supplies would get wet.

The missionary fathers then told the Governor that when they left the Province due to the French invasion, they had constructed a canoe which they left at a creek which was about a league distance on the other side of the river. His Lordship dispatched soldiers to see if it was still there. The search took two days, but they found it run aground at the creek. In light of this report His Lordship dispatched workers and oxen, which had been brought for such cases, and carpenters to make yokes and rollers. It was so difficult to transport it overland that it took four days to launch it in the river. The three companies crossed quickly thereafter. They were followed by the train, cattle, horses, and the rest of the battalion. Our total delay for all of this was of sixteen days.[229]

While at this campsite, the [Indian] captains of the Ranchería Grande came to camp. They brought some other Indians along. They were given clothing and other items. They were also fed during the days they stayed at camp. After having specially dressed the [Indian] captains, His Lordship sent clothing, knives and other highly appreciated items for the entire Rancheria. Soldier Nicolás de los Santos[230] took [the items] in two mule packs. He accompanied the [Indian] captains during the distribution, and because he is a great linguist, he learned of their great satisfaction.

Likewise, four Indians of the Texas and Ygodofas nations came [to visit] this campsite. They were also specially clothed and given presents so that they might return with news of the kindness with which the Spaniards were coming. They returned quickly to the [land of the] Texas.

After crossing everything, we [marched] for one league away from the [Trinity] river to the San Juan Creek[231] which, in order to prevent its swimming by the horses, His Lordship had previously ordered the construction of a bridge 15 varas long and three *and a half varas wide.*[232]

1 league

25th

On Friday the twenty-fifth it was necessary to delay in order to retreat the canoe which was up the [Trinity] river and taken out at a creek. It was thus assured for the return trip. On this day the *Cacique* of the *Aynay*[233] Nation arrived at camp.

He is recognized as the leader of all the Texas nations. He brought along eight chiefs and four maidens. One of the maidens was Angelina who had grown up at [Presidio] del Rio Grande and [Monclova] de Coahuila. She served as the interpreter, because she could speak the Castillian language as well as the Texas. The *Cacique*'s discourse was so laden with tears of joy due to the coming of the Spaniards that he was speechless for a while. He [finally] cried out that fifteen days before he had been informed of our arrival at the Trinity River. Becoming impatient of so much delay, he set out to meet us. He [also] said he really felt the absence of the Spaniards when the Padres and Captain Ramón left [the land of the] Texas. Since they had left him waiting, he also felt the [Spaniards] delay in returning. Had we delayed longer [the *Cacique*] would have gone to San Antonio looking for us.

The Governor replied with the corresponding attitude of good faith and gave him the love which His Majesty [may God protect him] has towards the Texas [Indians] and which is verified by *having sent the Spaniards to bring them peace*[234] and protect them from their enemies. [His Majesty] also sent the missionary Fathers to instruct them in *our Holy*[235] Catholic Faith.

[The Governor] then gifted [the *Cacique*] with a complete dress consisting of overcoat, jacket, and woolen breeches. He also gave him a silver headed baton naming him Captain and Governor of all the Texas Indians. [The Governor] also dressed the Indians and maidens who came in the [*Cacique*'s] company.

26th

The trip was continued on Saturday the twenty-sixth in a northeasterly direction over light forests of pines, pecans, oaks and vines. We passed two creeks and halted at Santa Efingenia Creek.[236] The day's journey was of four leagues. The march was followed by the [Indian] captain of the Texas and the other Indians. They were surprised at seeing so many Spaniards and so many cargoes and cattle.

4 leagues[237]

27th

On Sunday the twenty-seventh the Governor continued the march in an east-northeasterly direction over a great forest of pines, pecans and chestnut trees. We passed two creeks with running water. The march was concluded at Santa Coleta Creek[238] after having traveled seven leagues. The campsite was a beautiful clearing. From this point the President Father Friar Felix de Espinoza and the [Indian] captain of the Texas went ahead to prepare our arrival with the Indians at the original site of the first mission.

7 leagues

28th

On Monday the twenty-eighth the march was continued in the same east-north-easterly direction all the way to the site called San Pedro. The terrain and clear forests were as before. This is the site of the Presidio and mission established by the Spaniards in the first expedition of [sixteen] ninety and from which place they did not go beyond.[239]

3 leagues

The day's journey had been of no more than three leagues, because this is a comfortable site, and because no better one is known until the Rio de los Neches. On this day the Indians,[240] *maidens* and their children came to the campsite from their ranches which are nearby. They brought gifts of *corn,*[241] watermelons, pinole[242] and beans. They were affectionately received and dressed entirely by the Governor. They returned [to their ranches] very content and grateful.

The [Indian] captain of the Neches arrived at the same time with sixty Indians and maidens. They entered the camp firing salvos with their muskets. *The Governor*[243] received them with a great deal of pleasure. After making the peace sign which consisted of everyone smoking one pipe after mixing their tobacco with ours, the [Indian] captain told of the great pleasure he felt with the return of the Spaniards. He then offered his services and those of his people to continue the gratefulness [they felt] towards the benevolence of the Spaniards which they hope will continue. The Governor strongly assured him it would continue, and through the interpreter, Angelina, he then explained the reason for his coming.

[The Governor] suspended the act of clothing them until we arrived at Mission San Francisco where they live. He gave them enough meat and corn to eat that night and the following day.

That evening a Frenchman sent by Captain Luís de San Denis arrived from the capital of Texas where Mission Concepción used to be located.[244] He came to tell the Governor that if he were given safe conduct he would come to relay the orders he had received from Mobile as commander of the French Forces on this frontier. The Governor replied he could come in safety. [His Lordship] then dispatched the messenger immediately but he was not able to leave until the following morning.

3 leagues

29th

On Tuesday the twenty-ninth the Governor marched towards the northeast over a light forest with the same type of trees, hills and glens [as before]. We passed over the plain where the Presidio was first established in 1716, alongside a lagoon of sweet, spring water. The march was concluded at the edge of the Neches River after having traveled four leagues.[245] The Marquis ordered the construction of a bridge because the river was very flooded. Its construction took six days. It was 32 varas long and four and a half wide. It was so well done and so stable that it was given the blessing of the Church.

4 leagues

30th

On Wednesday the thirtieth there arrived [at camp] about 100 Indians, including women and children, who live at the Nacono[246] which is about five leagues away. They had been acquainted with the first mission, San Francisco de los Neches. Their [Indian] captain, who also happens to be their pagan high priest, is blind. It is presumed that after having been a chief for many years, he took out his eyes in order to become their high priest as is the custom among them. With the greatest of power and natural eloquence, and with signs, he made a long address to His Lordship expressing great happiness for the coming of the Spaniards. To prove his love further, he said that what he esteemed most were God, the sun, moon, stars and the Spaniards. [He added] that the water, airs and fire did not merit such a comparison.

Through the interpreter Nicolás de los Santos, the soldier who had come in the first expedition of Domingo Ramón and was very knowledgable in the [Indian] language and signs, the Governor replied that he highly appreciated the lovely expressions. He also explained His Majesty's motive in sending the Spaniards was to bring peace to this large Province, and to leave it protected with many Spaniards who would remain. And, that as long as it was necessary, many more would come to defend them from all their enemies. [They would also come] to establish for the [Indians] benefit, the Catholic Religion with preaching missionary fathers who were entering [the Province with the expedition]. Henceforth, the Indians would not have to fear any invasion.

[The Indian High Priest] was so happy that he raised his voice and gave a long and fervent address to all his people in which he repeated His Lordship's reply. He persuaded them to live as good friends of the Spaniards, and that they should join them in whatever wars might occur. He also asked them to hunt turkey, deer and bear and to bring all the food which they made and give them [to the Spaniards].

31st
On Thursday the thirty-first they brought the Governor tamales, watermelons, *corn*[247] pinole and beans. On this day His Lordship dressed all the men, women and children in wool, *flannel,*[248] sackcloth, hoods for the maidens,[249] and ribbons. He also gave them glass beads, hand knives, large knives, hoes, rings, mirrors, combs, awls, scissors, chain-links, and a blanket in *which the attire and all the other things were wrapped up and given to each.*[250] He gave the [Indian] captain a silver-handed baton and a dress of distinction as used by the Spaniards. His wife was given twice the amount given to the others. Everyone was very happy and content.

On the same day Captain Luís de San Denis arrived at camp after having swum his horse across [the river]. The Governor received him with the proper courtesy and respect. Since he said he was tired from the sun and the journey, His Lordship gave him the permission he sought to rest and to spend the night with the missionary father.

1st of August
On Friday the first after having heard mass, the Governor called for Captain Don Luís [de San Denis]. [The Governor] received him in the presence of the Lieutenant General and the captains. He was asked to reveal the reason *for his visit. He replied that as commander of the French*[251] forces on this frontier, he, if His Lordship was agreeable, would cease hostilities in obedience with the truce which had been amicably signed between the two crowns and published in Spain which, according to some correspondence he has received, is already in existence. His Lordship replied that in accordance with his orders, he would uphold the truce providing [San Denis] would evacuate the entire province of the Texas [Indians] taking all the Frenchmen with him to Natchitoches and not impede directly or indirectly the reinstatement of His Majesty's Forces to all of Our Lord's possessions inclusive of Los Adays. [San Denis] agreed completely even though his regret of losing Los Adays

was noticeable, because it is a site long sought by the French as an important communication point with their presidio at the Caudodaches[252] which opens the road to New Mexico. He argued that the site of Los Adays was unhealthful and that it could not be used for farming. However, we were not ignorant of the quality and healthfulness of the terrain, for it was there that the Mission San Miguel had been established[253] and which they, the French, had invaded. [San Denis] then took leave promising to retreat without delay with his people to Nachitoches.

2nd
On Saturday the second the Governor dispatched a detachment with the *President Father*[254] (Friar Isidro Felix de Espinoza) and Father Joseph Guerra to Mission San Francisco. Their horses swam (across the river). Another (detachment) with Fathers Gabriel Vergara and Benito Sánchez went to Mission Concepción. They went to re-establish the churches and living quarters *of the religious*[255] at both missions. To this day when the fathers were finally divided, they celebrated seven masses daily, and eight on feast days. On every Sunday they had celebrated a Mass with sermon which was much to everyone's satisfaction. Moreover, at all campsites *since San Antonio*[256] they had erected crosses to exalt it among so much idolatry and also to leave them as peace signs for the Apache Indians who hold them as so because they know that the Spaniards have been there.

3rd
On Sunday the third after finishing the bridge, all the people, equipment, *cattle*[257] and droves were taken across and marched east-northeast. The day's journey was of merely two leagues. We halted immediate to Mission San Francisco where the presidio had been established for the second time in 1716.[258]

2 leagues

4th
On Monday the fourth the Governor dispatched new reinforcements for the people who were working at Mission San Francisco so that a feast could be celebrated the following day for having re-established the Holy Catholic Faith which had been absent in the land of the Texas.

5th
On Tuesday the fifth after having learned that the church and living quarters for the missionary fathers were completed, the Governor and the entire battalion went

to re-establish Mission San Francisco de los Neches, commonly called "of the Texas." It was done with a very solemn High Mass celebrated by the Very Reverend Father, Friar Antonio Margil *de Jesús.*[259] During the course of the Mass there were salutes fired by all the companies as well as ringing of bells, blowing of horns and playing of drums. At its conclusion, the Indians who had observed it in admiration knelt before the altar at the first insistence of the president of the missions of the College of the Holy Cross of Querétaro, the Very Reverend Father, friar Isidro Felix de Espinoza.

[His Lordship] congregated everyone in the living quarters of the missionaries and in their presence, and in the presence of all the captains and officers of the battalion, in the name of Our Lord the King [may God protect him] he named the [Indian] Captain of the Neches. He gave him a baton of office and clothing as used by the Spaniards. He was unanimously acclaimed by all the Indians.

[The Governor] then completed by clothing *158*[260] men, women *and children.*[261] They were very happy because never before had they received so much of so many different things. Through the Father President he then told them that the main reason for this trip had been the zeal *and desire*[262] of His Majesty to save their souls and bring them under his Royal and benign protection and to defend them from all their enemies. [His Lordship] made them realize that the [French] were only interested in their chamois, buffalo, and horses and especially in their women and children for slavery. He also told them that Our Lord the King [may God protect him] did not ask for anything. Instead, [the King] would gift them in abundance as they had just witnessed. The Governor himself had been careful not to accept even a chamois as a gift lest it be seen as a sign of recompense.

His Lordship made it clear to them that all [the King] wanted was for [the Indians] to enter the fold of the Church. For this reason it was necessary for them to congregate and unite at the said Mission and form a pueblo like the Spaniards. [The Governor] named the pueblo San Francisco de Valero with the admonition that it should not be like before when they did not congregate. This time they were to carry it out without fail.

The said President Father relayed all this to them for he is very experienced in their language. They replied unanimously their willingness to do so as soon as they reaped the maize crop which they had on the field. And so that they might do so while the Governor was at Los Adays, the President Father asked His Lordship to give the Indians possession of the land and necessary water rights for their permanency. He agreed to do so and gave them in name of His Majesty. After having finished all the acts of possession, [His Lordship] installed Father Friar Joseph Guerra of the College of the Holy Cross as missionary, having been selected on the recommendation of the Father President of the said college. [The Governor] told [Father Joseph Guerra] he had full confidence that his zeal would allow the conversion of all those souls as soon as possible.

The march was thence continued towards the northeast and east-northeast through a clear forest of heavy oaks and mulberry trees. We crossed two creeks and two plains until we arrived at a creek with running water which is at the beginning of another plain larger than the preceding ones. We made halt at this site because it was late due to the fact that we had spent *almost*[263] half a day at the mission. His Lordship named the said creek and campsite Nuestra Señora de las Nieves.[264] The day's journey was of four leagues.

4 leagues

6th

On Wednesday the sixth we continued in the same direction through the same type of trees and plains. We crossed a creek and then a plain and after about two leagues we encountered a small *river*[265] with permanent running water.[266] The river rises so high during most of the year that the Indians keep a canoe there for crossing it. This time, however, it was not necessary. *His Lordship*[267] named it Santa Barbara because it did not have a name. It is less than half a league distance from Mission Concepción de Nuestra Señora. In order not to damage the crops in the nearby ranches, the Governor decided to camp a league farther on, where the presidio of Domingo Ramón was located[268] at the time the missions were abandoned. The day's journey had been of five leagues.

That same afternoon *His Lordship*[269] sent a reinforcement of workers to help repair the church. Only the church of this mission was not entirely *ruined.*[270] [The reinforcement] also went to construct the living quarters of the padres.

As soon as His Lordship arrived, the Indian Juan Rodríguez told him that he had learned that Captain Don Luís de San Denis, after returning from the Neches River where he had seen His Lordship, had camped for about three days some seven leagues from that campsite with the Cadadoche Indians and other [Indian] nations from that Province. [They were the same Indians] which he had convened since last winter to sound out the Bay of Espíritu Santo and from there go to San

Antonio. All of this [shady business] had been cleared away with the coming of the Spaniards.

5 leagues

7th

On Thursday the seventh in accordance with the Governor's order, we marched with great care so as not to damage the maize. The Indians were very pleased with the order but even much more pleased later on when they saw the order of the march. On this day the church was completed and the artillery was prepared for the fiesta.

8th

On Friday the eighth the Governor and the entire battalion including the two companies of Don Alonso de Cárdenas and Don Juan Cortinas, went to the mission. As soon as he arrived, His Lordship gifted the Governor of the Texas [Indians] with the best attire of blue cloth heavily embroidered in gold and a waist-jacket of gold and silver. The attire included the remainder of the corresponding items so as to complete the dress.

The *ten*[271] companies were formed in three straight lines in front of the church. The artillery was positioned between the church and the battalion so as to fire the three salvos during the Mass which was sung by *the President Father of the missions of Nuestra Señora de Guadalupe* [*de Zacatecas*],[272] the Very Reverend Father Friar Antonio Margil de Jesús. The Very Reverend Father Friar Isidro Felix de Espinoza, *President Father of the College of the Holy Cross* [*of Querétaro*][273] delivered the sermon with great eloquence and tenderness at seeing the reinstatement of the mission and the Holy Catholic Faith.

Many Indians from different Nations attended the ceremony. Among them were about 80 from the Cadadoches who were under French rule and had attended the previously mentioned convocation with the Texas [Indians]. Their Governor lives at this *mission.*[274] They were all very impressed with the artillery and with the *orchestrated salvos*[275] of the companies. They seemed very surprised, yet pleased, at seeing so many Spaniards. After Mass all the captains of the Indian Nations as well as many Indians and maidens went to see His Lordship at one of the houses of the missionaries. Each of the Texas [Indians] brought a small gift of the plates which they eat. They consisted of beans, *corn,*[276] pinole and tamales. [His Lordship] displayed great esteem towards their good faith, and once again offered them the love which the Spaniards had always held for them. He assured them that this time many in his company had come to stay, and they should not fear that as before, they would be abandoned. [His Lordship] left them satisfied that they would be defended from all their enemies.

Being aware of the great following of Cheocas, the Captain of the Texas [Indians], the Governor then asked him to bring his people together, all men, women and *children*,[277] so that they might be given clothing and other items. He also wanted them to understand the intentions of His Majesty in sending so many Spaniards. [Cheocas] replied that they were dispersed over many far ranchos, but that he would bring them together after leaving only the most necessary numbers at their homes.

His Lordship then celebrated the day by hosting all the priests and captains to a sumptuous meal. After lunch, the President Father asked for the [official] title of possession for his college and for the Indians. Solemnly, His Lordship gave the same to the said Priest as well as to [Indian] Governor Cheocas. The missionaries for this mission were identified as the said President Father and Father Gabriel Vergara.

That evening His Lordship returned with all the companies to the campsite.

9th
On Saturday the ninth His Lordship dispatched a lieutenant with a detachment with Father Friar Benito Sánchez[278] to Mission San Joseph de los Nazois which is eight leagues distant to the north from the Mission de la Concepción.[279] He is the missionary assigned to the mission [San Joseph]. They went to construct the church and living quarters of the priests, for they were both in ruins.

8 leagues

10th
On Sunday the tenth the Governor sent another detachment with the Most Reverend Friar Antonio Margil de Jesús, President of the missions of the College of our Lady of Guadalupe, and two other religious. They went to erect Mission Nuestra Señora de Guadalupe de los Nacogdoches, for not even traces were left of the church or the living quarters of the priests. It was about eight leagues distant from the campsite.[280]

11th
On Monday the eleventh the captain-governor of *all*[281] the Texas [Indians] gathered all the people of the *Aynais*[282] and the eighty Cadadoches who came with them and who belong to Mission Concepción. Many of them came carrying their muskets to the campsite of His Lordship. After giving them the same arguments as the other Indians for congregating themselves in a pueblo. They offered to do so after reaping their crops. [His Lordship] then gave them some clothing and entirely dressed 400 Indians as was his custom. He also distributed some items which they like very much. He gave each and every single one some knives, scissors, combs, mirrors, *awls,*[283] *large knives,*[284] *pieces of steel for striking flint,*[285] ribbons, women's necklaces, chochomite,[286] belts, glass beads, ear rings, and rings. His Lordship also dressed two [Indian] captains who came with the Cadadoches giving each a bundle of clothing. He also gave them some of the described merchandise to distribute among their people. The Governor saw fit to do so in order to make them friendly to the Spaniards and also because they are confederates of the Texas [Indians]. They were all very satisfied and contented.

12th
On Tuesday the twelfth the battalion was left at this campsite so that the horses might rest. The Governor went on with one company to Mission San Joseph de los Nazonis which is eight leagues away. The Indians of that place received His Lordship with many happy manifestations.

13th
On Wednesday the thirteenth the reinstatement of that mission was celebrated with a High Mass and repeated salvos by the company. After Mass the Father President and the [Indian] captain of the Nazonis were formally given title of possession with the same solemnity as at the other missions. With all the Indians, women, boys and girls belonging to the mission being present, His Lordship then installed their recognized captain by giving him a silver-handed baton. Through an interpreter [His Lordship] then explained the reasons for his coming and asked them to unite in a pueblo as he had done at the other missions. *They offered to do so.*[287]

His Lordship then clothed the [Indian] captain in a complete[288] Spanish dress as used by the Spaniards. He then gifted everybody else, without excluding anyone, with the same items as at the previous missions. He left some items to be distributed among those not present with Missionary Friar Benito Sánchez who is encharged of this mission. [The absent] had been left guarding the fields and houses. This had also occurred at the other missions. They were all so very happy that all day long they brought squash, watermelons, *corn,*[289] and pinole. Three hundred Indians were clothed at this mission.

14th
On Thursday the fourteenth the Governor returned to camp to re-join the battalion.

15th
On Friday the fifteenth, following a very early Mass celebrating the Feast of the Assumption, His Lordship installed the company of Captain Juan Cortinas which is composed of 25 men at their old Presidio which is a league distant from the missions. They will protect and assist the missions.

[The Governor] and the battalion marched off towards the east-northeast over a light forest of pecans, pines and oaks until arriving at a very clear site which has a deep ravine where camp was made. Because it did not have a name, it was called Arroyo de la Assumpción de Nuestra Señora.[290] The day's journey was of four leagues.

4 leagues

16th
On Saturday the sixteenth His Lordship continued the march in the same direction of east-northeast over the same type of terrain and forest to the site of Mission Nuestra Señora de Guadalupe de Nacogdoches which belongs to the college of Zacatecas. The day's journey had been of four leagues.[291]

4 leagues

17th
On Sunday the seventeenth the church and living quarters of the priests were completed with the reinforcements given by His Lordship from the battalion.

18th
On Monday the eighteenth the completion of the church was celebrated with a *High*[292] Mass with a sermon by the Most Reverend Father Friar Isidro Felix de Espinoza, President of the missions of [the College of] the Holy Cross [of Querétaro]. The nine companies formed in rows in front of the church with Cárdenas' company *between them,*[293] fired the salvos as at the other missions. After Mass,

Friar Antonio Margil de Jesús, President of the missions of [the college of] Our Lady of Guadalupe, asked His Lordship for title of possession in name of his college and of the Indians. His Lordship gave him the title with all due solemnity. Father Friar Joseph Rodríguez was appointed missionary [for this mission].

All the Indians of all ages being gathered, *the Governor*[294] then clothed their recognized Indian Captain in a complete suit of English cloth and all corresponding items including a silver-handed baton and official title of [Indian] Captain. He [the Governor], then dressed all the other [Indians] as was his custom and distributed the gifts as he had done with the Indians at the other missions. He explained the reason for the expedition and urged them to congregate *in a pueblo.*[295] They promised to do so in a lengthy oration full of many happy expressions. The Governor then solemnized the fiesta by hosting a banquet for all the priests and captains.

Three hundred ninety Indians were clothed.

19th

On Tuesday the nineteenth the Governor continued the march in an east-northeasterly direction with some variances due to the meanderings of the road. The entire [march] was over ravines, light forests of pines, oaks, and pecans. Several creeks were crossed, and it was necessary to construct bridges at two of them. Halt was made near the last creek at a plain where there is a small lagoon which His Lordship named San Bernardo.[296] The day's journey was of six leagues.

The Most Reverend Father[297] Margil and a *detachment*[298] struck ahead from this point to construct Mission de los Dolores which is next.

6 leagues

20th

On Wednesday the twentieth His Lordship continued the march in the same direction as before and over the same type of terrain and trees as the day before. A *large creek*[299] or river was crossed. It carries much water when flooded. It was already known as Todos Santos. The battalion camped along its bank after having marched eight leagues.[300]

8 leagues

21st

On Thursday the twenty-first the Governor continued the march in the same direction of east-northeast over broken land with creeks and forest until about a quarter league beyond the place where Mission Nuestra Señora de los Dolores de los Adays used to be located.[301] There were no traces left [of the old mission]. *Reverend*[302] Father Margil had found a better site along a creek and spring which begins nearby. This site is higher and clearer and has a large plain for sowing.

The day's journey was of six leagues.[303]

6 leagues

22nd

Friday the twenty-second was utilized for building the church by using all the necessary people.

23rd

On Saturday the twenty-third the fiesta was held with all the solemnity as at the other missions. There was a High Mass and all the companies fired a salute. Thereafter, title of possession was given to the President Father Friar Antonio Margil and to the Indian Captain. [His Lordship] clothed the latter as he had done with all the other [Indian] captains. He also dressed all the Indians and maidens in the same manner as at the other missions. *The Governor gave them the necessary orations and they replied as at the other missions.*[304] The fiesta was enlightened with an abundant feast given by His Lordship for the priests and all the captains.

Father Joseph Alvadadejo remained [assigned] to this mission where one hundred and eighty Indians were clothed.

24th

On Sunday the twenty-fourth the Governor left a detachment behind to finish the construction of the church and to build the living quarters of the priests. The march then continued towards the east with some variances to the *east-northeast*[305] over terrain covered with pecan and pine trees, and over ravines, clearings and some creeks with running water. His Lordship *ordered a halt*[306] near a lagoon which he named San Bartholomé after having marched five leagues.[307]

His Lordship dispatched an express to San Antonio with several orders and especially to speed-up the battalion's convoy. A general salvo was fired at prayer-time in honor of the Prince's birthday.[308] Also on this day, the express which His Lordship had sent to His Excellency arrived with the reply[309] in which the latter thanked him for the discovery which the former offered to make at his own expense of the route from Vera Cruz to La Bahía del Espiritu Santo which the French call San Bernardo. [The discovery of] this bay would aid the Province and

[His Excellency] had already issued the orders for the bilander to sail from Vera Cruz.

In the same express, His Lordship's agent informed him that he had already made arrangements for the freight costing 3,500 pesos and that all during the month of July it would sail from Vera Cruz with all which had been asked for.

5 leagues

25th

On Monday the twenty-fifth His Lordship continued the march towards the east-northeast over land broken with high hills and ravines. [The terrain] has *heavy*[310] forests and some creeks over which some bridges were made due to the muddiness. *Halt*[311] was made at a lagoon which His Lordship named San Luís and which is about one league distant from the crossing of the Sabine River.[312] The day's journey was of seven leagues.

7 leagues

26th

On Tuesday the twenty-sixth the Governor proceeded in the same direction as the day before. We crossed the Rio de San Francisco de Las Sabinas[313] even though its water was higher than the *breast-plate.*[314] Over half a day was spent in crossing [the river] for the approach had to be fixed because it was long and muddy. The afternoon was spent in crossing the small pools and muddy places on the opposite side of the river and which during winter are impassable. Camp was made on a hill next to a creek which His Lordship named San Nicolas de Tolentino.[315] The day's journey was of three leagues.

3 leagues

27th

On Wednesday the twenty-seventh His Lordship marched in the same direction over hills, ravines and forests of pines, pecans, oaks and some chestnuts and medlar trees. [We also crossed] several creeks. We reached a large creek which *His Lordship*[316] named Santa Rosa de Lima.[317] The battalion camped on its opposite bank on a clear plain. The day's journey was of six leagues.[318]

6 leagues

28th

On Thursday the twenty-eighth *His Lordship* continued the march in the given direction[319] over the same type of terrain *with hills, ravines, and forests of pines, oaks, and clearings*[320] *as the day before.*[321] [Some] creeks were crossed, and it was necessary to construct some bridges to cross some of them. His Lordship camped between a lagoon and an arroyo which he named San Augustin.[322] The day's journey was of eight leagues.

8 leagues

29th

Before departing on Friday the twenty-ninth, the Governor increased the picket with a detachment so that they might open an approach and exit to the creek due to its impenetrable dense brush. They were also to construct a large bridge.

After receiving news that all was done, His Lordship set out in the same direction as the day before and over clear plains and light forests of medlars, pecans, pines and oaks. Upon arriving at the site where mission San Miguel de los Adays used to be located, His Lordship discovered it was too uncomfortable as a campsite for the battalion because it was too low and subjected to flooding if it rained. Also, there was no running water in the creek.

Scouts were sent out in different directions and half a league *further on*[323] they found a spring which flowed into a large plain. This was chosen as the campsite. The journey was of three leagues.[324]

3 leagues

30th

On Saturday the thirtieth, after not being able to find a single Indian at Los Adays, His Lordship dispatched parties in different directions. On the following day they reported finding the Rancherías nearby at about ten or twelve leagues distance. As per instructions, they informed the Indians of the coming of the Spaniards. The Indians were extremely happy, and their captain-general said he would *immediately*[325] gather his people and come to see His Lordship.

1st of SEPTEMBER

On Monday the First a Frenchman arrived at camp bringing a letter from the commandant at Natchitoches, Captain Rerenov. The letter, which His Lordship later sent to the Viceroy, complimented His Lordship on his arrival. It also stated that when Captain Luís de San Denis returned from the [land of the] Texas in mid-August, he left for Mobile by way of the Natchitoches River which the French call Rivera Roja. He went to report to his governor of the coming of the Spaniards. The commandant [who brought the letter stated] he did not have authorization to allow us to settle at Los Adays. Therefore, [he asked] His Lordship to remove himself until the return of Captain Luís [de San Denis].

In light of this ambiguous proposal, the Governor immediately convoked a War Council where it was resolved that on the following day the Lieutenant General Don Fernando Pérez de Almazán should go to Natchitoches with Captain Don Gabriel Costales. They were also to observe the approaches to the island where the presidio is located and the type of fortifications which it had just in case war should break out. [This was especially true] for the French had seen the forces brought by His Lordship.

In his reply to the commandant, [His Lordship] stated that since affairs of war could not be dealt with satisfactorily with a pen, he was [therefore] sending his Lieutenant General to clearly express His Lordship's determination in coming. On the basis of this letter, the Lieutenant General extended his conference with the [French] commandant telling him that the objective behind the coming of the Governor was to occupy the land of the Adays as had already been done with the land of the Texas. He added [the Governor was] to re-establish the Mission of San Miguel [de los Adays] and construct a presidio on that frontier at the most convenient site.

The [French] commandant replied that he did not have specific orders to agree to this or to prevent it. [He added] that he knew of the truce which existed in Europe between the two crowns and that he would uphold it in America if His Lordship agreed to it. With this [act] the conquest of that entire Province was completed. It was based on the condition that both parties would uphold the truce and that all which the Arms of His Catholic Majesty had possessed in that Province would be returned to the rule of Our Lord the King [may God protect him]. [Finally], the Governor was to fortify whatever site he chose on that frontier.

The Marquis immediately set out to select a site to establish the presidio. Even though he dispatched scouts over the entire territory, and even though he personally set out to reconoiter the terrain, he did not find a better site or a more convenient one than the place where he was already encamped. [This site] is on the Camino Real to Nachitoches and *seven*[326] leagues distant thereof.[327] He chose this site because the rest of the terrain was too dense and its forest too shady. This site, however, has good ravines where the mission can be established near the presidio and sufficient land for the Spaniards and the Indians to use for planting. Also, there is a spring or water on a nearby rise.

It is a site which dominated the entire area. His Lordship outlined and immediately began to construct a hexagonal fortress. Three bulwarks were excluded and three others were added [in their place]. By luck, each of these protected two curtains. Because each curtain was 55 varas [in length], the bulwarks sloped not only to the ground but to the very quarters of its 100 man garrison. Thirty of these soldiers were to be constantly occupied in the care and protection of the horses and cattle. Even though [the fortress] only had six artillery pieces, [this was still acceptable] because the water was only half a musket shot distance away. However, water will be sought within the fortress through a well. Crowbars had to be used in laying the foundations and clearing the site for the fortress. The forest around it is very heavy and dense. This too will be cleared so that it may be as it should be so that the enemy may not approach hidden [in its density].

1st of SEPTEMBER

On September first the chief of the Adays came with many Indians all showing great merriment at the coming of the Spaniards. They were affectionately received by the Governor and given gifts as had been done with the other [Indian] captains of the Texas Indians. [The Chief] explained to the Spaniards the great pleasure which he felt with their coming because all of the Indians of that country wanted to live under their protection. They desired this because when the French invaded Mission San Miguel de los Adays, they and the Nachitoches Indians displayed hostility towards them for lamenting the retreat of the Spaniards. [The French and the Nachitoches] took some captives including men, women and children at the time of the [Spanish] retreat. For this reason they had been forced to abandon the country and move to more distant and harsh land from which they had come to see the Governor. There were more than 400 men, women and children and His Lordship made them very happy with all the clothing and gifts which he distributed among them. He dressed them as he had done at the other missions. His Lordship then assured them of the protection of Our Lord the King for which reason a presidio was being established in that frontier with 100 men near the reestablished Mission San Miguel. [The Indians] promised to congregate therein.

Among the news which His Lordship investigated in that country was that given by the Indians concerning a nearby saltpit. Being that its discovery was as useful as necessary, His Lordship dispatched a lieutenant with a party of 20 soldiers and 25 mules to search for it. They brought [the mules] loaded with salt-dirt which was so good that half of it could be yielded with little work. They found it 15 leagues distance from where the presidio was erected.

The restoration of the mission which was to be established a quarter league away, was celebrated on the feast day of the Archangel Michael at the [presidio's] church. The dedication of the presidio and church were celebrated on October 12, the feast day of the apparition of Our Lady of Pilar de Zaragosa whom His Lordship had chosen as patroness and spiritual protector of the frontier. Both fiestas were celebrated most solemnly and joyfully, and with the greatest artillery salvos possible. The companies which had been formed on the parade grounds during the Mass, also fired repeated salutes. The Mass was sung by Doctor Don Joseph Codallos y Rabál who had previously blessed the temple and fortress. The image of Our Lady of Pilar was carried in procession, and her cult was extolled with a *very devout*[328] and eloquent sermon by the Most Reverend Father, Friar Antonio Margil. The fiesta was concluded with a splendid banquet which His Lordship hosted for the priests *and Captains.*[329] He gave brandy to the troops, and they in various *festive*[330] dances, plays and *masquerades*[331] displayed their happiness.

In mid-October *the Governor*[332] received the good news of the arrival of the bilander at La Bahía del Espíritu Santo on the feast day of the Nativity of Our Lady. [This was the bilander] which His Lordship had contracted at a cost of 3,500 pesos to open the route from Vera Cruz to La Bahía. It brought 350 loads of flour and 150 loads of maize.

The news was celebrated in a manner befitting both the discovery of the important route and the arrival of the fresh provision which had immediately been forwarded on the mules which His Lordship had kept at San Antonio awaiting the shipment. The 200 loads of flour and other items arrived at a very good time because the Governor was very worried because there was no corn other than for the Indians at Los Adays or [at the land of the] Texas. Therefore there would not be enough food for the troops if misfortune struck the convoy.

Forty loads arrived on the twentieth of October. The rest [arrived] at the beginning of November accompanied by a party [escorting] 300 head of beef and 400 sheep which had come from the frontier of the Kingdom of [Nuevo] Leon which is 340 leagues distant from Los Adays.

The great lake of Los Adays begins at about a league distance from the site where the presidio was located. The road which goes to Natchitoches has a ten league detour [around the lake] to where the road crosses the Cadadoches River.

There are approximately 60 leagues between the two presidios. The nearest part of the lake to Natchitoches is only four leagues away.[333] Moreover, all year round the lake had an abundance of different kinds of fish as well as a large variety of ducks of different sizes all during winter.

In the land of the Adays [Indians], there are bears, deers, pecans and medlar trees. The Indians store large supplies of these items as well as bear lard, which is very delicious, for winter.

The Governor dispatched an express[334] to the Viceroy informing him that the fortress and [soldiers'] quarters had been finished on All Saints' Day.[335] He also informed him that he was leaving 100 men for the garrison at the presidio including the 31 who had brought their families. Six artillery pieces, war and food supplies, and all other necessary items for the maintenance of the people who were also left [at the presidio]. Even though no more than 90 loads of flour were left, [the Governor] made plans to forward 100 more loads from the second convoy of which His Lordship had been informed was enroute from La Bahia to [the land of the] Texas.

Having finished everything, the Governor then ordered all to be ready to begin the return trip on November 12. A very heavy sleet storm started the day before [the march was supposed to begin]. Even though the tree limbs were thick, they were so heavily covered with icicles that some limbs began to fall off while other trees just toppled over exposing their roots. They fell so easily that within 24 hours some 200 must have fallen in the campsite alone, and some 2,000 in its vicinity. Many of the horses and mules upon which they fell were killed. Thanks be to God an officer was merely hurt by a tree which fell on his shoulder while he slept. His life had been in imminent danger.

Even though the weather let up after three days, we were not able to gather the horses and mules until the seventeenth, on which day the march began. The march was difficult from the very first steps. The horses were dropping dead because of the great debilitation they had suffered during the cold spell. From Mission Dolores which is 30 leagues from *the Presidio*[336] of Our Lady of Pilar, many of the soldiers began to march on foot.

An express from Mexico City arrived at the next mission of Our Lady of Guadalupe. It was a reply to the one sent from this site by the Governor to the Viceroy during the coming [to this country]. It also contained a copy of the Real Cédula which His Excellency had received by way of a mail vessel. The Cedula was dated on May 6, 1721, at Aranjuez in which Our Lord the King [may God protect him] saw fit to approve all the decisions which His Excellency had made concerning this expedition which he had entrusted to the Governor. [The King] again ordered that war was not to be made against the French in recovering the Province. This information, and especially the news of the King's good health was celebrated with repeated salvos.

His Majesty also ordered the Province to be defended with Presidios [to be established] at the most convenient sites. This applied particularly to La Bahía del Espíritu Santo which had now been occupied for a year *and garrisoned*[337] by 40 soldiers. The Viceroy ordered the Governor to augment this garrison with *50*[338] soldiers and to select the best under his command.

29th

On the twenty-ninth His Lordship arrived at the Texas Presidio where he outlined the fortification for a garrison of 25 men. It was a square design with only two bulwarks at the opposite corners each of which covered two curtains. Each [curtain], including the demigorge, was sixty varas [in length].

The site [for the presidio] is a very good one. It is on a rise overlooking the entire area. Creek Nuestra Señora de la Assumpción which has permanent running water passes nearby.[339]

His Excellency delayed only three days at this site because he was worried that the flooded rivers might slow down the march. He sent out scouts, and they reported that the Santa Barbara River, which is located between missions Concepción and San Francisco, was flooded. Therefore, he ordered a bridge of 30 varas in length to be constructed. The bridge facilitated the crossing without any delay whatsoever.

9th

On December 9, at Santa Efigenia, His Lordship encountered the awaited second convoy from La Bahía. On that same day he sent to Los Adays 100 of its loads of flour and other provisions. The rest was kept for maintenance during the journey.

His Lordship decided to make the return trip via the lower road through the Monte *Grande*[340] because the Trinity River was carrying about half a vara of water. He had also learned from some soldiers whom he had sent out to scout [the area] that the Brazos de Dios River had a good crossing. An Indian guide then led the 17 league journey through the Monte Grande passing over clearings and light forests.

The diary of the return trip was not kept because the route was over a known road, and because the daily marches were irregular and of one, two or three leagues. From the Texas Presidio onward, most of the people were marching on foot due to the bad weather, terrible ice storms, and the death rate of the horses and mules. At San Juan Evangelista Creek[341] which was located right before the entrance to the Monte Grande, His Lordship was forced to leave 80 loads [of provisions] guarded by an escort of 20 soldiers.

His Lordship realized his arrival at San Antonio would be delayed. Therefore, from the Trinity River he sent ahead ten soldiers to bring the necessary provisions which [His Lordship] feared would be lacking enroute. [The soldiers] returned with 32 cargoes and met [the battalion] at Encadenado[342] campsite which was four leagues away from the San Marcos River.

His Lordship was also informed that sixteen huts belonging to the soldiers *at San Antonio*[343] had burned. The granary with 700 bushels of corn and the flour supplies [had also burned] not even leaving an ear of corn. He then ordered the mule packs which he had left at Saltillo be brought with all haste lest something happen to the bilander [also]. [The mule packs] had been left at Rio Grande with 200 loads of flour and 1,000 bushels of corn. The mule packs arrived very promptly, and it became necessary to leave enough supplies at that presidio for the maintenance of the troops as well as for the continuation of the march. [His Lordship] also dispatched expresses to Guadiana and other places asking for a herd of 800 horses as soon as possible.

The *troublesome*[344] journey continued with the captains and other officers also marching on foot. The Governor also marched on foot on several occasions to join them in their suffering.

His Lordship[345] arrived at San Antonio on January 23, with the happy consolation that the multitude of misfortunes had striken only the horses and mules. Their mortality rate had been so high that out of 5,000 horses no more than 50 returned. Out of 800 mules which had set out, only 100 returned. However, not a single soldier was lost. Even two [soldiers] who had left Los Adays in poor health arrived well and sound at San Antonio. His Lordship dispatched an express to the Viceroy informing him of all this as well as of the return trip.

The Governor was informed through some letters he had received that the herd of horses which he had ordered would be delayed for about a month and a half. [In the meantime,] His Lordship realized that the Presidio de San Antonio was defenseless and also exposed to fire as the soldiers had recently experienced for living in thatched roof huts. Therefore, His Lordship attempted to construct an accident-proof fortress made of adobe. After ordering the cutting of the necessary lumber for the church, stores and quarters, His Lordship selected a better site than that on which the presidio used to be located.[346] [This new site] was between the San Pedro and San Antonio rivers.

It was first necessary to clear the land by cutting down many trees. A great number of people were then put to work making adobe [bricks]. His Lordship then outlined the fortress as a square with four bulwarks so that if ever the soldiers were out on a campaign, and there were few left [at the presidio] and it came under attack, then these few could protect the position by using only two opposing bulwarks. Two curtains [of the presidio] could be defended from each bulwark. Each curtain is only 65 varas in length.

His Lordship encouraged the abundant planting of corn for the maintenance of the soldiers and friendly Indians who were constantly coming to see the Spaniards. The irrigation ditch which His Lordship had ordered constructed at his own expense from the San Pedro River [sic] could very well irrigate the two leagues of fertile land which it encloses between itself and the San Antonio River which it enters below the presidio. This area which actually looks like an island, is widest at the new site of the presidio which will be 30 varas from the San Pedro River [sic] and 200 varas from the San Antonio.[347]

The reply to the express which His Lordship had sent from Los Adays on November 4, arrived on March 8. It contained letters from the Viceroy in which His Excellency thanked the Governor profusely in many expressions of gratitude. He also approved all which His Lordship had done in Texas for the recovery of the Province, as well as for the *fortification*[348] which he had left at Los Adays for protection [of Texas].

On the tenth of the said month [of March] after having previously selected a good site between the two missions of San Antonio and San Joseph,[349] the Governor proceeded to place [Indian] captain Juan Rodríguez in possession of the mission for himself and for the Indians who accompanied him from the Ranchería Grande. Even though there were no more than 50 families, [Juan Rodríguez] promised and assured [the Governor] that the rest of his following would come as soon as they learned that a mission had been established for them.

Full title of possession was given [to the Indians] in care of Father Friar Joseph González who received it in the name of the College of the Holy Cross of Querétaro under the name of [Mission] San Francisco Xavier de Nájera.[350] All the officers of the battalion attended the ceremony. On this same day, His Lordship clothed Indian Juan Rodríguez in a complete suit of English cloth as used by the Spaniards.

With the first herd of horses which arrived, His Lordship dispatched the 50 soldiers who had been assigned to La Bahía. They had volunteered from all the companies of the battalion, but only the very best were selected and placed under the command of Captain Don Gabriel Costales.

Because not enough horses had come, His Lordship was not able to depart until the sixteenth of the said month [of March]. On this day a special detachment of 40 men from all the companies left with Doctor Don *Joseph*[351] Codallos y Rabál and captains Don Thomas de Zubiria, Don Miguel *Colón y Portugal,*[352] Don Manuel de Herrera, and Don Pedro de Oribe.

The direction of the march was south to Mission San Joseph y San Miguel de Aguayo which is about two leagues distant and thence south-southeast for the remainder of the journey to the Salado River.[353] The day's journey was of four leagues over light forests of oaks and evergreen-oaks.

4 leagues

17th[354]

On Tuesday the seventeenth His Lordship continued the march in the same direction of south-southeast over the same type of terrain and forest. We passed several clearings with good pasture until we reached the Aguila campsite.[355] There are several pools here which keep water all year round. The day's journey was of four leagues.

4 leagues

18th

On Wednesday the eighteenth the Governor continued the march towards the south for about two leagues and thence took some variances towards the east for the rest of the journey to the Cíbolo River which was about eight leagues [total].[356] It was very difficult land with sand and heavy forests of evergreen-oaks, mesquites, and oaks. There was no water in between with the exception of a very small puddle.

8 leagues

19th[357]

On Thursday the nineteenth the Governor continued the march towards the east-southeast over terrain with the same type of trees and mesquites as before. There were some sparse clearings [along the route]. The day's journey to the San Cleto creek was of seven leagues.[358]

7 leagues

20th[359]

The march on Friday the twentieth did not begin until the afternoon, because many horses had been lost during the rain storm which had occured in the morning with much thunder and lightning. The horses were not recovered until midday. We thence marched two leagues towards the east over the same type of terrain as the day before to a creek which His Lordship named San Joachín because it did not have a name.[360] There are many turkeys [in this area].

2 leagues

21st

On Saturday the twenty-first His Lordship continued the march towards the east-southeast for three leagues over a heavy forest of oaks and evergreen-oaks. Thence [we marched] another three leagues east-northeast over a beautiful plain without trees or brush. We also declined our direction towards the east for another three leagues over an open country. The day's journey was of nine leagues [total] to a creek which His Lordship named San Benito because it did not have a name.[361]

9 leagues

22nd

On Sunday the twenty-second the Governor marched towards the east-southeast over an open country with some broken spots for about six leagues. We thence declined our direction towards the east for another three leagues following the banks of the Guadalupe River until we found a crossing over some rocks.[362] Since the river bed was very wide and it carried over a vara of water, it became necessary to divide each load into three parts. His Lordship selected a campsite on the opposite side of the river. The day's journey was of nine leagues.

9 leagues

23rd

On Monday the twenty-third His Lordship continued the march in the same direction *of east-southeast*.[363] For the first half league we marched through a light forest of oaks and evergreen-oaks. The rest of the route was over a very level terrain where the horizon was expended. We thence declined our direction towards the east for four leagues. We concluded the day's journey on the bank of the San Joseph River after marching seven leagues.[364]

7 leagues

24th

On Tuesday the twenty-fourth the Governor marched in an easterly direction over the same type of open land covered with flowers. After crossing two creeks with plenty of water, we declined our direction towards the east-southeast for five leagues. After having marched nine leagues [total], His Lordship arrived at the Presidio of Our Lady of Loreto de la Bahía del Espíritu Santo.[365]

9 leagues

Nothing was accomplished during the first eight days because the Governor was confined to his bed due to his poor health aggravated by the hardships of the expedition which he had begun to suffer in San Antonio. Moreover, those days were devoted to the Church because it was Holy Week. This afforded great consolation to all because it was the first time they could observe them decently in the presence of Our Lord in the Repository.

On the second day of Easter, April 6, His Lordship began to outline the foundations of the Presidio in accordance with the orders of Our Lord the King [may God protect him] at the site where the French had theirs under LaSalle from 1684 to 1690.[366] All the Frenchmen except three men and one girl had been killed by the Indians. The French had buried their artillery, and it was later recovered by the Spaniards and sent to Vera Cruz. The hole [in which the artillery had been buried] could still be seen. It fell within the site where the presidio was to be established. They also burned their powder at this site.

On digging the foundations for the fortress, we found nails, pieces of gun locks and fragments of other items used by the French. The foundation for the octagonal fortress was laid in 15 days. It was a covered moat and had only four bulwarks *because the present garrison is no more than 90 men. However, its garrison will be enlarged because it is an important port.*

In place of the other four bulwarks, His Lordship outlined four serpentine extentions[367] as well as a tower in the angle formed by the curtains. Each curtain was forty-five varas in length.

After completing this chore, His Lordship proceeded to establish Mission Espíritu Santo de Zúñiga which was located near the presidio. All this time a number of Indian families had come telling the Governor that many more [Indians] would settle here if they saw them congregated [in a mission]. There was no doubt that they would do so because they had shown much pleasure and happiness with the gifts and other items distributed among them by the Governor as at the other missions. It was also known that these Indians were more docile [than the ones who had killed the French], and they would be happier cultivating crops and their own souls. They lived in more misery than the other Indians. Their diet consisted solely of fish and [they] had no clothes. On their own they asked the Governor to baptize three of their children. He did so and then much to everyone's pleasure, he gave more presents to the children's parents. The missionary assigned to the mission, Father Friar Augustín Patrón, of the college of Our Lady of Guadalupe de Zacatecas, baptized the children.

All round the presidio there are beautiful fields of clear land and *flowers*[368] which, in light of our brief and short observation of one year, is very fertile. It also has some beautiful strips of land for raising horses and all types of cattle. Moreover, there is an abundance of deer and turkey. This is especially true on the San Antonio-La Bahía road.

Leaving Captain Don Joseph Ramón who is assigned to that presidio encharged with finishing the construction of the fortress, His Governor set out for San Antonio. He arrived on April 26, still in poor health. His Lordship said, however, that he was very happy to have enjoyed good health during the time he had served His Majesty in this expedition. The only thing left was for him to return with all his people to Coahuila. He was not able to do so until May 5, because the last herd of horses did not arrive until April 30. *The rest of the horses had come while His Lordship was at La Bahía.*[369]

The new Presidio de San Antonio could have been finished in the meantime had it not been for the continuous rains. Not only was it impossible to work for three weeks, but the 30,000 adobe bricks which His Lordship had ordered made while he went to La Bahía were all destroyed in the rains. Nonetheless, most of the task and *25,000*[370] bricks were completed. A large amount of material was successfully gathered for the construction by the 40 Indians whom His Lordship hired at his personal expense. All continued working.

The Governor left [San Antonio] on the fifth of the said month. After two days journey, at the site called La Pita, the horses stampeded during a very stormy night. It took all of the following day to recover them, and even then, 80 horses were lost. The march was continued to the Rio Grande without obstructions or delays. The river was carrying more than a vara of water.

Two days journey past the presidio [de Rio Grande], at the site called San Diego the horses again stampeded during a very stormy night. It took four days to recover them and 40 horses were lost.

We crossed the Rio Sabinas with much difficulty and delay even though it was not carrying more than half a vara of water. His Lordship and the remainder of the troops were discharged on the thirty-first [of May] as per the *Viceroy's*[371] orders to do so as soon as they returned to this town and concluded the expedition. [His Lordship] ordered the troops be paid two extra months above their second year and that they be given all they needed for the return trip [to their homes] which they began on June 12.

The Arms of Our Lord the King [may God protect him] have been covered with glory in this expedition because with a mere threat this extensive Province and all which the French had claimed has been re-established to the Dominion of His Majesty. Moreover, many and numerous [Indian] Nations which exist in the 200 leagues from the town and Presidio of San Antonio to Our Lady of Pilar de los Adays, have been brought under the obedience of His Majesty. [The Presidio of Los Adays] was established and the 80 leagues [from San Antonio] to La Bahía del Espíritu Santo have been opened.

Had there been a battle during this expedition, the captains, subalternates, and soldiers would have done their duty. The spirit of devotion they have displayed is second in a soldier only to valor. They have endured all types of setbacks in the long and exhausting marches. They bore up against the severe river floods and indifferently shrugged off all types of weather sometimes extremely hot and at others freezing cold in winter. They walked through the most vehement changes of coldness as well as sweltering heat. At times it seemed as if Hell had conjured all its power in furious, never-before-seen storms of that country where we had gone to congregate many souls within the fold of the Church and re-establish our Holy Catholic Faith in [Hell's] tyrannical empire. [Our Church] had not only been abolished and villified, but its temples had also been demolished and profaned. Even though this outrage might have not been repaired, it was at least compensated in part by all the souls from so many different languages and Nations who have now been saved in their old age. Seeing themselves on their death bed, [the Indians] have asked for baptism [for themselves and] for their children whom their parents realize were in danger. They continue to do so in the nine missions which the Governor has re-established as well as at [Mission] San Antonio de Valero.

All the kingdoms of New Spain are now protected by this buffer which has been added in this vast Province. [The kingdoms are also protected] by the string of presidios which had been established from Los Adays, Texas and [La] Bahía, and by fortifying the [Presidio de] San Antonio to where the Spaniards retreated when the French occupied the rest. This latter presidio is at the entrance to Texas and had never had any fortifications.[372]

In this military engagement expanded over 26 months the Governor has shown his innate love and zeal for the Royal Service by executing all the decisions and orders of the Viceroy promptly and correctly. Of no less importance has been the care and measures he took to maintain the troops at his own expense in those distant deserts. The supplies and provisions had to be transported over 400 leagues.

With the greatest complacency he has shown his love for sowing the Gospel Truth among so many souls who live in the sad shadows of mankind. [The Governor] also displayed his intention of returning the Province to its rightful ruler. It is also known that Our Lord the King [may God protect him] has a Catholic, Christian zeal to extend his dominion over the entire world and thus bring Christ, the Sun of Justice, for all to see.

Our guiding light in this enterprise has been Our Lady of Pilar whom the Governor selected as guide and patroness. As a shield on the Texas frontier he left this Tower of David so that she might protect it just as she had done when the Most Holy Virgin left her image and column of Non Plus Ultra at Zaragoza which was then the edge of the known world of the Spanish people. The Plus Ultra has likewise been placed [on this frontier] to protect the most remote people who have been discovered in America by the Spaniards.

In an act of thanksgiving His Lordship concluded the expedition yesterday with a beautiful and solemn fiesta in honor of Our Lady. We implored not only the maintenance of that Province, but also for the addition of all [other Provinces] where the sun might shine to the Crown and dominion of our Catholic Phillip, for in this manner they will come into the Kingdom of God which is praised by all creatures for all eternity.

[Signed] at Santiago de la Monclova, capital of the Province of Coahuila, New Estremadura, on June 21, 1722.

Br. Don Juan Antonio de la Peña[373]

I, *Doctor*[374] Don Joseph Codallos y Rabál, Qualifier and Commissioner of the Holy Office [of the Inquisition], ex-Visitor General and Synodal Examiner of the Bishopric of Guadalajara, Vicar and Ecclesiatical Judge of the Real and Mines of San Gregorio de Mazapil and town of Saltillo and Vicar General of the Province of Texas, New Phillipines, etc. etc.;

Hereby certify that the diary which has been written and signed by Bachelor Don Juan Antonio de la Peña, Chaplain-Major of the Battalion of San Miguel de Aragón, of the trip and expedition which the Marquis de San Miguel de Aguayo has executed to the Province of the Texas to recover it, re-establish its missions, and establish a protective wall with the establishment of the Presidios of Adays, Texas and La Bahía del Espíritu Santo and by which these dominions of New Spain are protected, IS TRUE, CORRECT, AND IN EVERY DETAIL WRITTEN WITH UTMOST EXACTITUDE. I was an eye-witness to all these events, for I accompanied the Marquis from when he left the Rio Grande del Norte until he returned to this town of Santiago de la Monclova, capital of the Province of Coahuila. In order to give credence to this I hereby affix my signature on this the 22nd of June, 1722.

Dr. Don Joseph Codallos y Rabál[375]

signed before me
Antonio de Espronzeda
Notary Public

The Spanish Presidios Of Texas And La Salle's Fort St. Louis

The second Marquis de San Miguel de Aguayo, Don Joseph de Azlor y Virto de Vera, was not only wealthy, but educated and well read. As a well bred Spanish officer and gentleman, he obviously read and studied Sebastien Leprestre de Vauban's *Manuel of Siegecraft and Fortification.* This becomes very apparent in the floor plans of the presidios designed by Aguayo. The presidios and their designs, interior and exterior defenses were 17th century French fortifications!

The French military engineer's *Manual* was written between 1667 and 1672. His second *Manual* was written in 1706. Both manuals had wide circulation in manuscript form. Both dealt with siege and attack of fortifications. Surprisingly though, the former *Manual* was not published until 1740. The latter was published in 1737. The second Marquis de San Miguel de Aguayo must have read the manuals in manuscript form.

Aguayo's reasoning for using the French designs was not only understandable, but quite appropriate and correct. Leprestre de Vauban had authored the best guide for siegecraft and fortification. The French were using his plans and designs in France, Europe, Canada and Louisiana. The French were also threatening Spanish Texas. Like a good military officer, Aguayo merely adopted the enemy's strategy in siegecraft and fortification. Hence the French designed Spanish presidios.

Ironically though, the presidios were never built; at least not according to design and specifications. At Los Adaes, for instance, de la Peña recorded there were no rocks, not even little ones, for constructing the presidio. Nonetheless, Aguayo laid the foundation and opened the trenches for a wooden stockade. Presidio Nuestra Señora de los Dolores was altered to have only two bulwarks instead of four. Again, due to lack of stone the exterior wall was nothing more than a wooden stockade. Presidio Loreto was properly designed and its foundation laid and trenches opened. However, there is no record of its construction. By 1726, the presidio had been moved to the west bank of the Guadalupe River. In 1749 it was moved again to present day Goliad, Texas. Meanwhile, the Presidio San Antonio de Bexar was apparently never completed. Perhaps Aguayo did not know that adobe could not be used in the San Antonio area. The dirt was too rich and the rains too frequent. The missionaries and settlers knew this and constructed their structures of caliche.

The second Marquis de San Miguel de Aguayo nonetheless deserves a special place in Texas Military History. His intentions, vision and attempts [if not accomplished] with regard to construction of the presidios were unmatched. After the threat of a French invasion had subsided, other less enthusiastic Spanish officers did away with Aguayo's plans. Brigadier Generals Pedro de Rivera [1727] and Teodoro de Croix [1776] and Colonel Hugo de O'Conor [1773] all changed or did away with Aguayo's work. They all came later and times had changed. LaSalle, St. Denis, the French threat and the second Marquis de San Miguel de Aguayo had become historical memories.

The floor plans of the presidios designed by Aguayo appear on the following pages. They have been analyzed and interpreted by this author on the basis of de la Peña's descriptions and Sebastien Leprestre de Vauban's *Manual of Siegecraft and Fortification*. May they remain a monument to the intentions and enthusiasm of the second Marquis de San Miguel de Aguayo, Don Joseph de Azlor y Virto de Vera.

Presidio San Antonio De Bexar In The Province Of Texas New Kingdom Of The Phillipines

The presidio is six leagues away from the boundary line of Coahuila. The Marquis de San Miguel de Aguayo outlined the fortress and left all of its foundation and a great deal of the building completed. Expecting it to be finished shortly, he left the necessary lumber and other material at the foot of the structure.

The fifth part of the curtain which corresponds with the demigorge of the bulwarks was not given so that the 54 man garrison may better defend the fortress. Also, there are usually very few men left to protect the fortress when the soldiers go into the field. He designed it square shaped for the same reason, that is, so that a few men may defend it from two opposing bulwarks. Once the garrison is augmented then they may construct a covered walkway, moat and revelins to better protect the curtains.

The Church is located as shown (on the plate). The entrance is on the south. The storehouses are next to the main entrance. The quarters of the Captain and the officers are at the bulwarks. The remainder are the quarters for the officers. Each have their respective corrals as shown (on the plate) with dotted lines.

The San Pedro River (sic) is 30 varas from the fortress. The San Antonio River is 200 varas distant. The presidio has been placed further from the latter because it has a great deal of trees and the San Pedro has none.

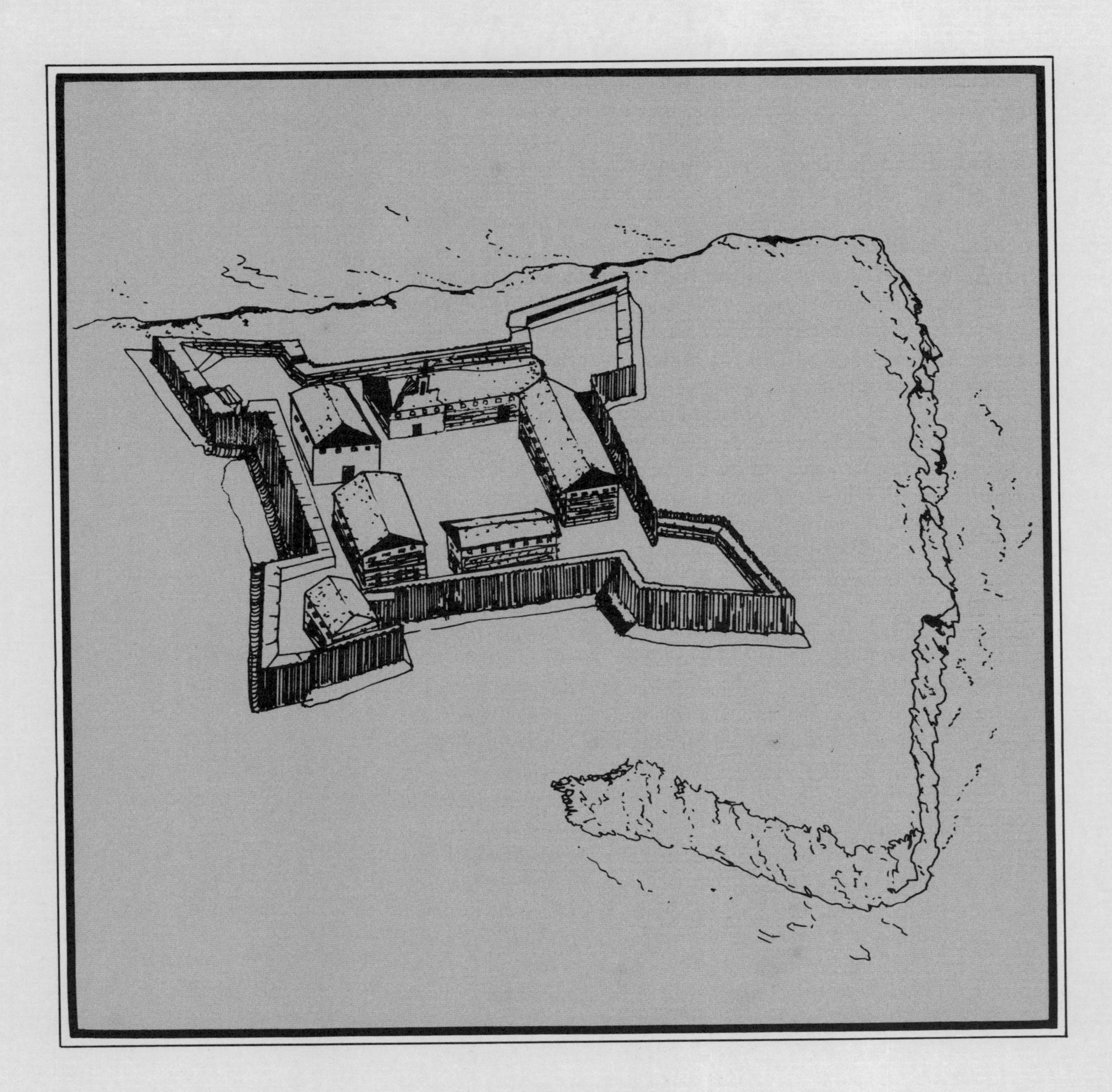

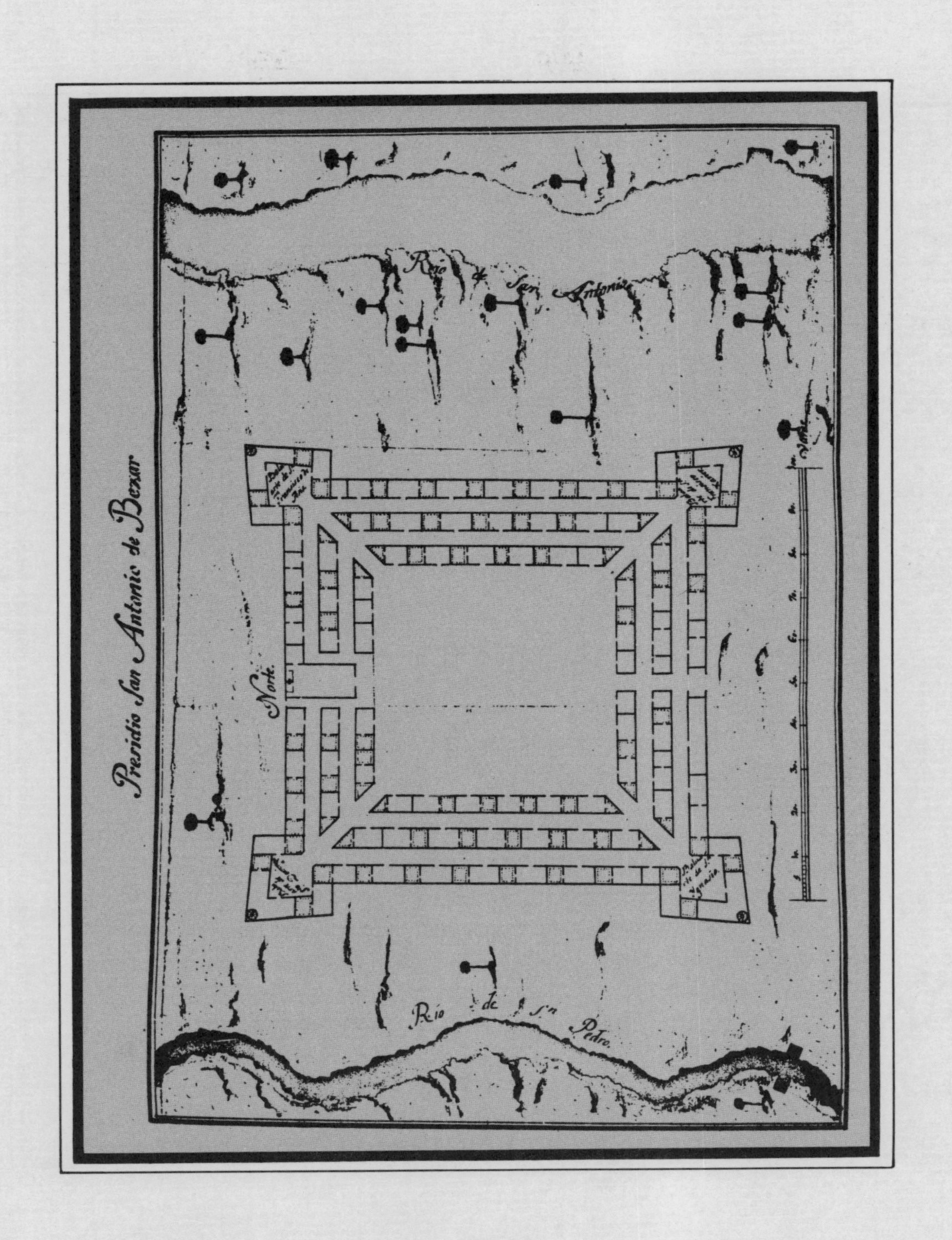
Presidio San Antonio de Bexar
Rio de San Antonio
Rio de Sn Pedro
Norte

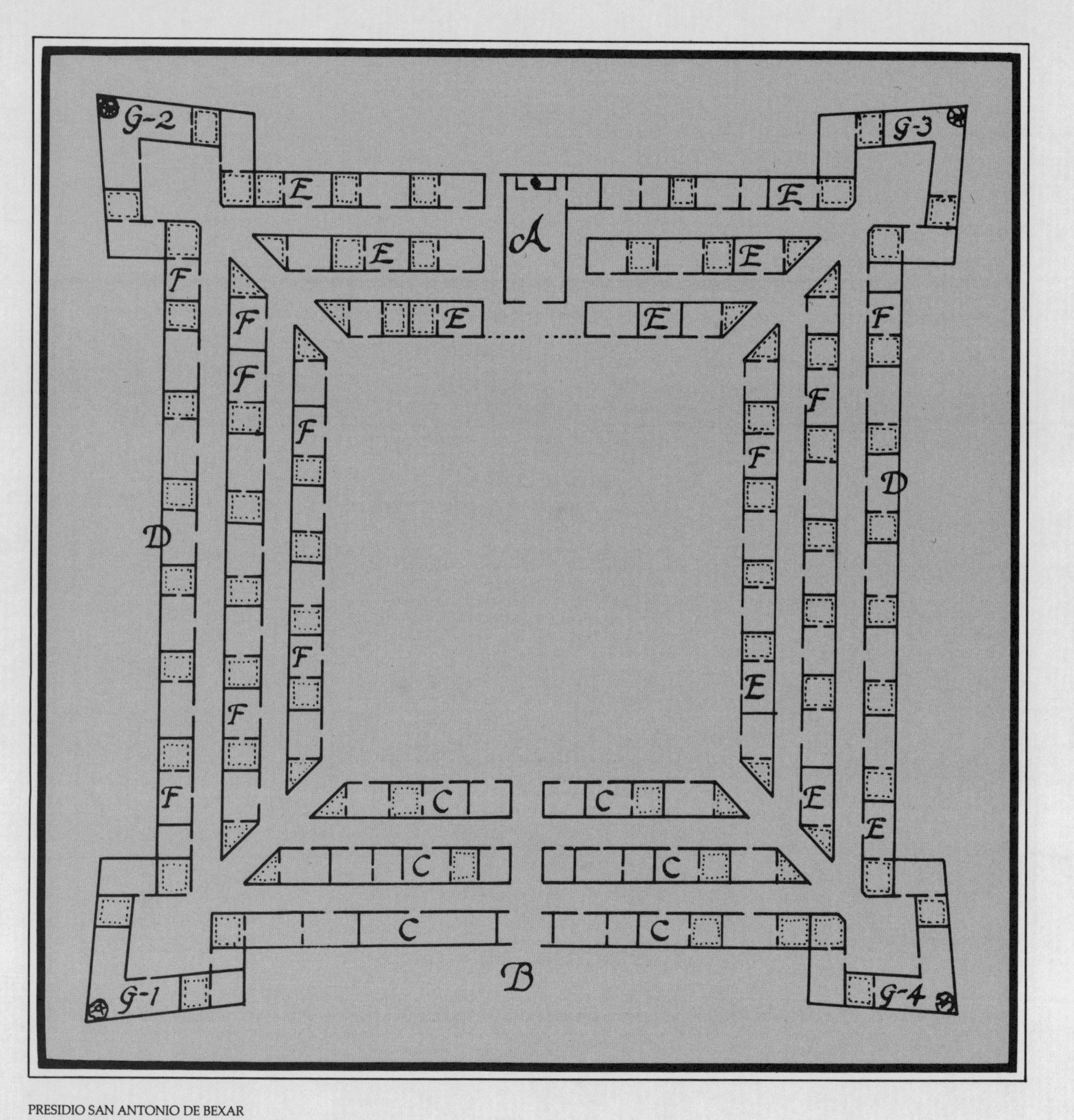

PRESIDIO SAN ANTONIO DE BEXAR

A. CHURCH
B. MAIN GATE (facing south)
C. STOREHOUSES
D. CURTAIN
E. OFFICER'S QUARTERS
F. ENLISTED MEN'S QUARTERS AND CORRALS
G-1. BULWARK SAN YGNACIO
G-2. BULWARK SANTO DOMINGO
G-3. BULWARK SAN FRANCISCO DE ASSISI
G-4. BULWARK SAN FRANCISCO XAVIER

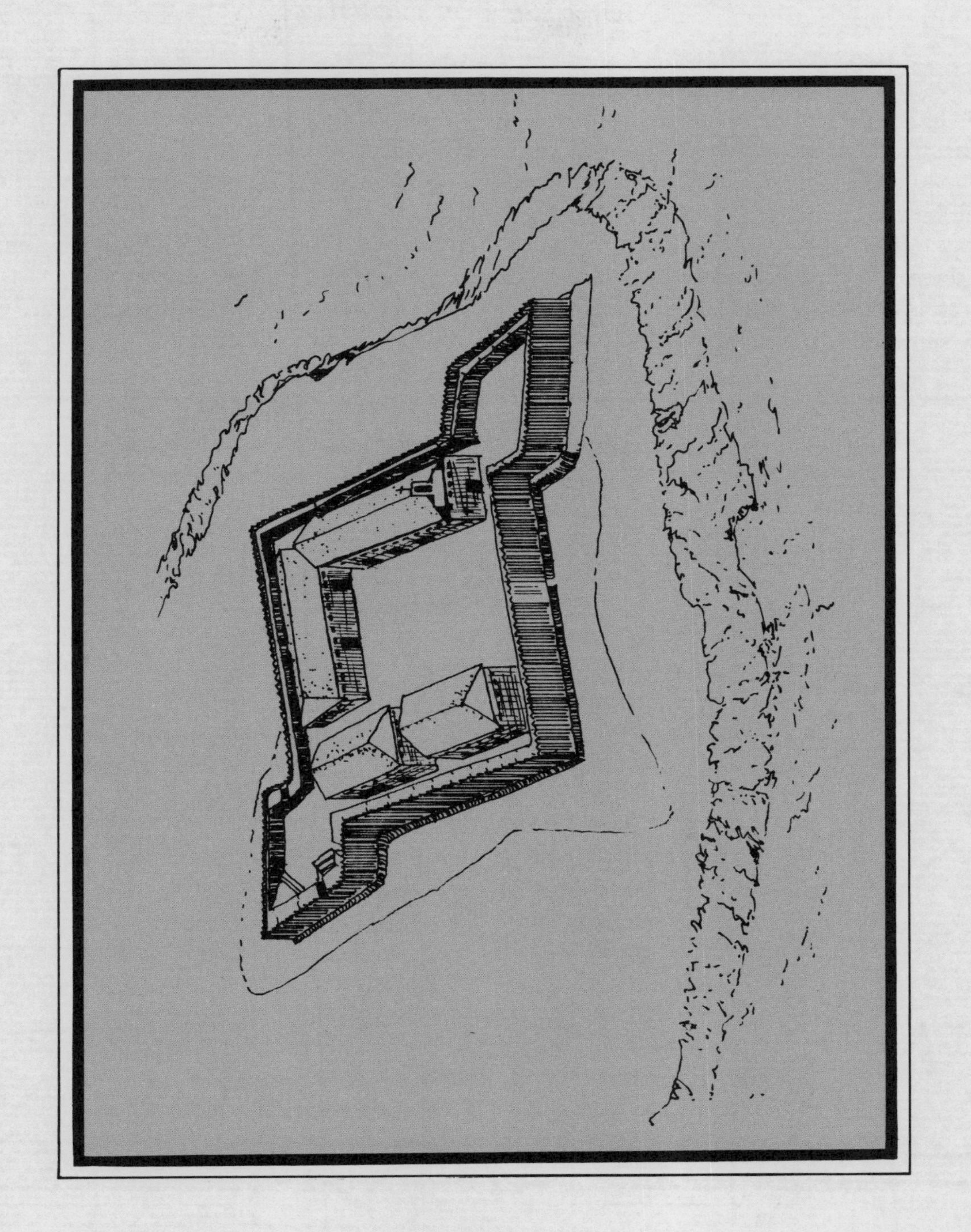

Presidio De Nuestra Senora De Los Dolores

The Presidio is adjacent to Mission Nuestra Senora de la Concepcion which is located at the center of the land of the Texas Indians. It was outlined and erected by the Marquis de San Miguel de Aguayo. Two of the bulwarks corresponding to the square shaped fortress were omitted to accommodate its 25 man garrison. In this manner they will be able to better defend the fortress.

It is located on high ground free of all obstacles. It has a great plain to the south and west. A large valley to the north begins at the curtain and bulwark San Jorge. The creek is about 25 varas distant or a small musket shot distance. The storehouses are on the same side as the church, and next to them is the captain's quarters.

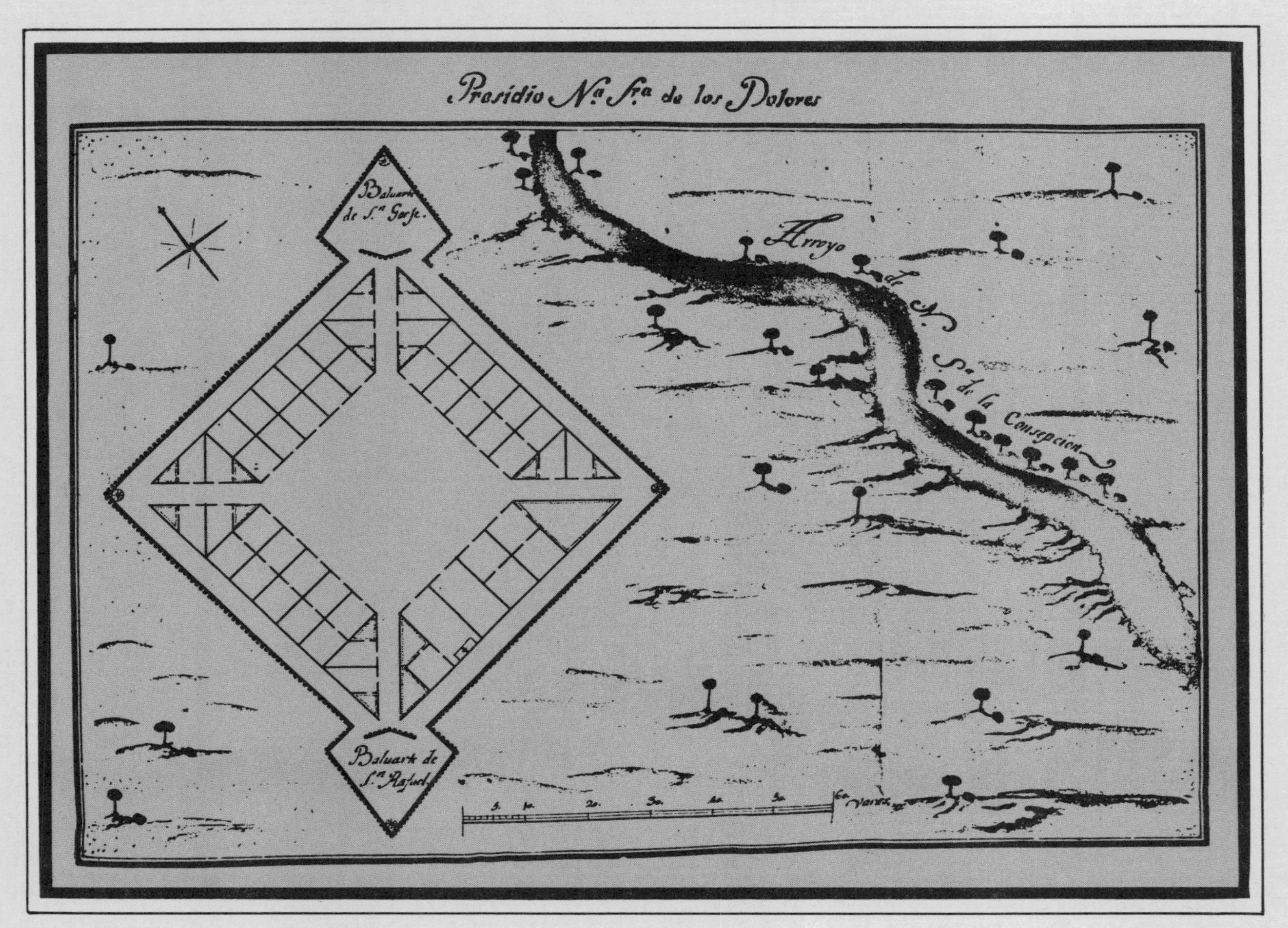

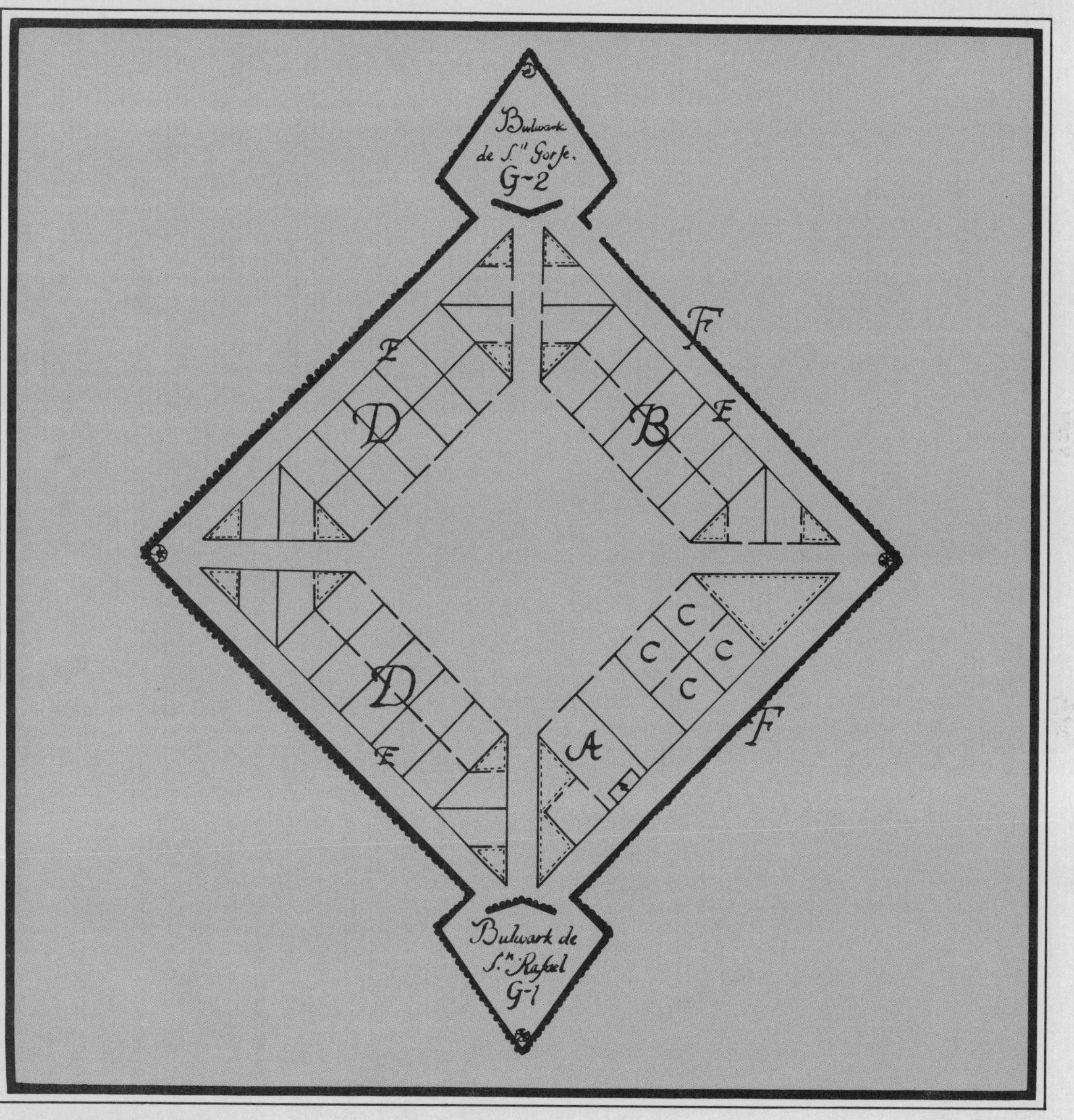

PRESIDIO N.S. DE LOS DOLORES

A. CHURCH
B. OFFICER'S QUARTERS
C. STOREHOUSES
D. ENLISTED MEN'S QUARTERS AND CORRALS
E. CURTAIN
F. PALLISADE
G-1. BULWARK SAN RAFAEL
G-2. BULWARK SAN JORGE

Presidio Nuestra Senora Del Pilar De Los Adaes On The Frontier of Texas New Kingdom Of The Phillipines

The fortress was outlined and finished by the Marquis de San Miguel de Aguayo on the first of November, 1721. The proper and regular measurements were not given to the foundation and the flanks of the bulwarks because three of the sides were excluded from the hexagonal. This was done so that the 100 man garrison may better defend the fortress. It was also done to accommodate the site on which the pallisade is located which is surrounded by a forest.

The fortress overlooks the surroundings from its elevated position which is 16 varas away from water which is to be found in a ravine a musket shot away. However, a water well will be dug within the fortress. Also, the pallisade will be replaced with adobe because there are no stones nearby; not even small rocks. The moat outlined as surrounding the curtains will be extended to cover the bulwarks.

The living quarters of the missionary fathers are next to the church. The commandant's quarters and the storehouses are on the section immediate to the church. The quarters for the junior officers are next to the gate. The remainder are corrals and quarters for the soldiers.

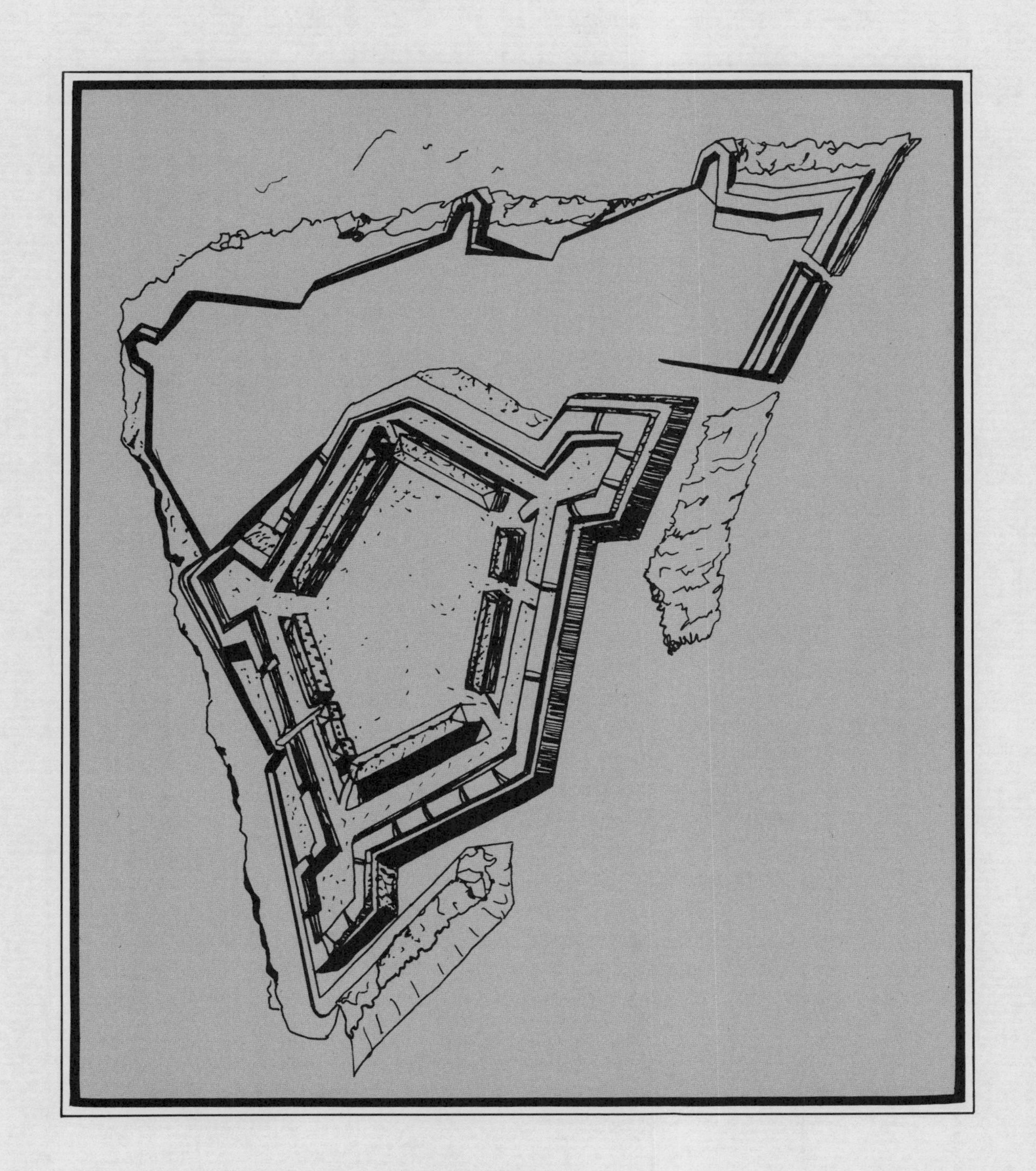

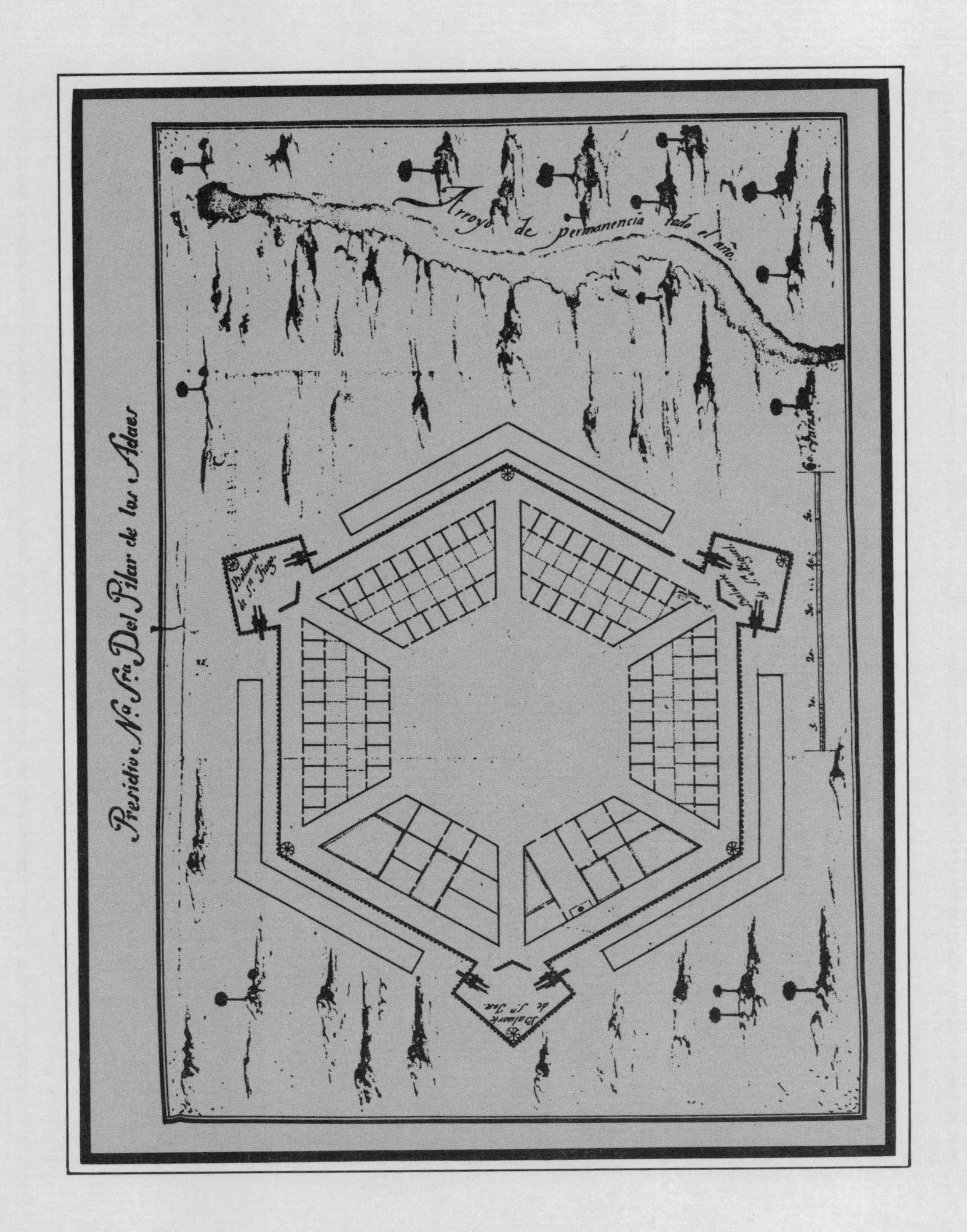
Presidio Nª. Srª. Del Pilar de los Adaes
Arroyo de permanencia todo el año

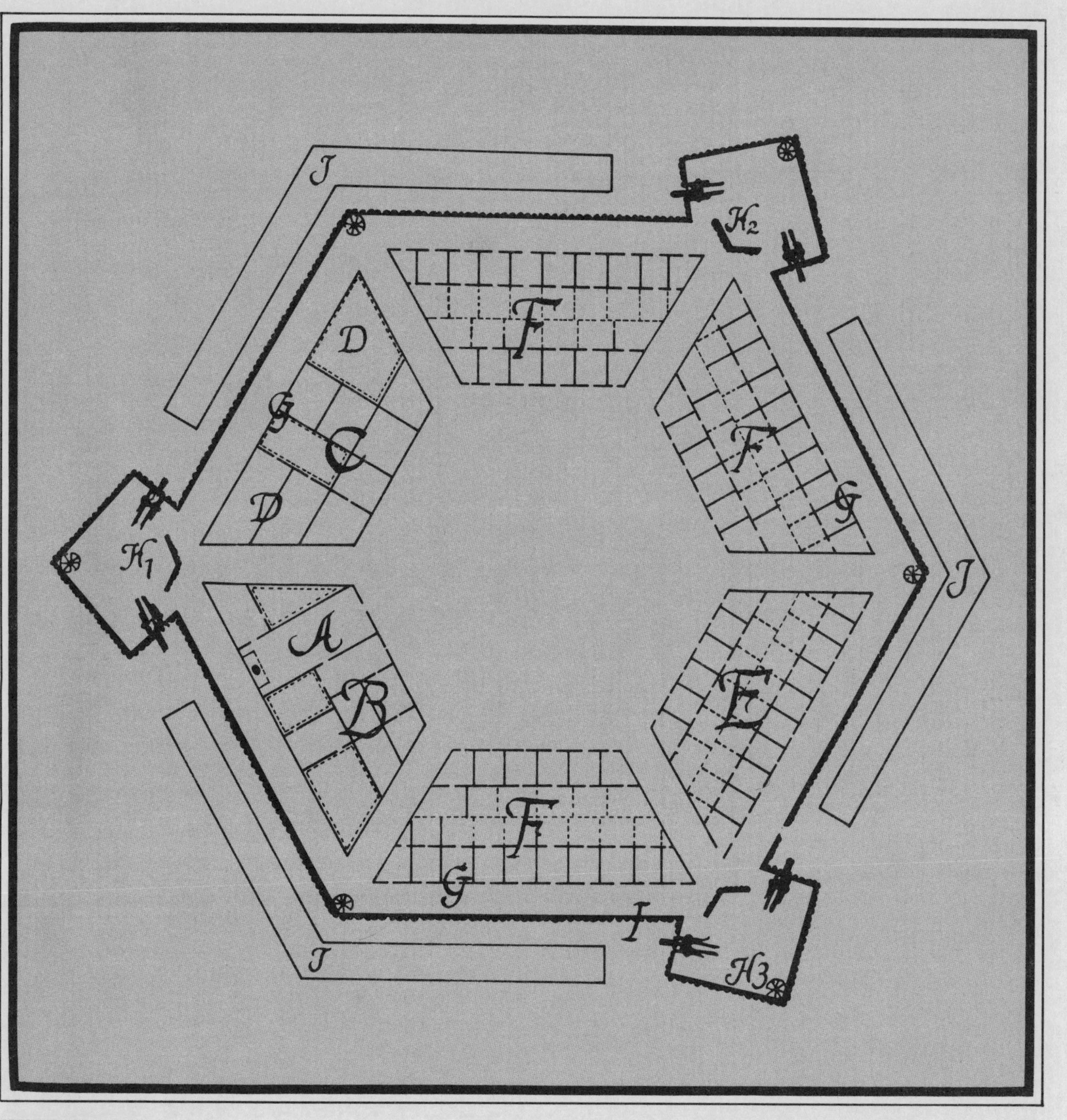

PRESIDIO LOS ADAES

A. CHURCH
B. PRIEST'S QUARTERS
C. COMMANDANT'S QUARTERS
D. STOREHOUSES
E. JUNIOR OFFICER'S QUARTERS
F. ENLISTED MEN'S QUARTERS AND CORRALS
G. CURTAIN
H-1. BULWARK SAN JOSE
H-2. BULWARK SANTIAGO
H-3. BULWARK SAN MIGUEL
I. PALLISADE
J. TRENCHES (to be connected and thus become a Moat.)

La Salle's Fort St. Louis
by
Alonso De Leon
April 22, 1689

". . . The settlement was composed of a small wooden fortress and six very weak small houses. All were made of wood and mud. The roofs were made of buffalo hides. They were all very weak for any type of defense.

What little jewelry the inhabitants possessed had all been sacked. Over 200 books written in the French language were strewn over the yard. Their pages had been torn out. All were rotting due to the frequent rains which had obviously occurred. The enemy (Indians) had made a horrible ruin of all which they (the French) had possessed. . . . The enemy Indians ravaged not only the inhabitants, but their arms as well. Over a hundred broken arquebuses could be seen near the houses. They obviously mistook them for canon and struck them against the artillery pieces breaking the stocks, grips and hammers. Three bodies were found and one of them seemed to have been a woman because a skirt was still clining to the bones. The rest of the body had been eaten by (wild) animals. All the bones were collected and buried with a Solemn High Requiem Mass.

About eight new iron artillery pieces of six and eight pounds were found between the fortress and the houses. Some were still on their carriages. Others were on the ground. Some broken locks for the arquebuses were found near the houses. Three swivel guns without their breeches were also found. . . ."

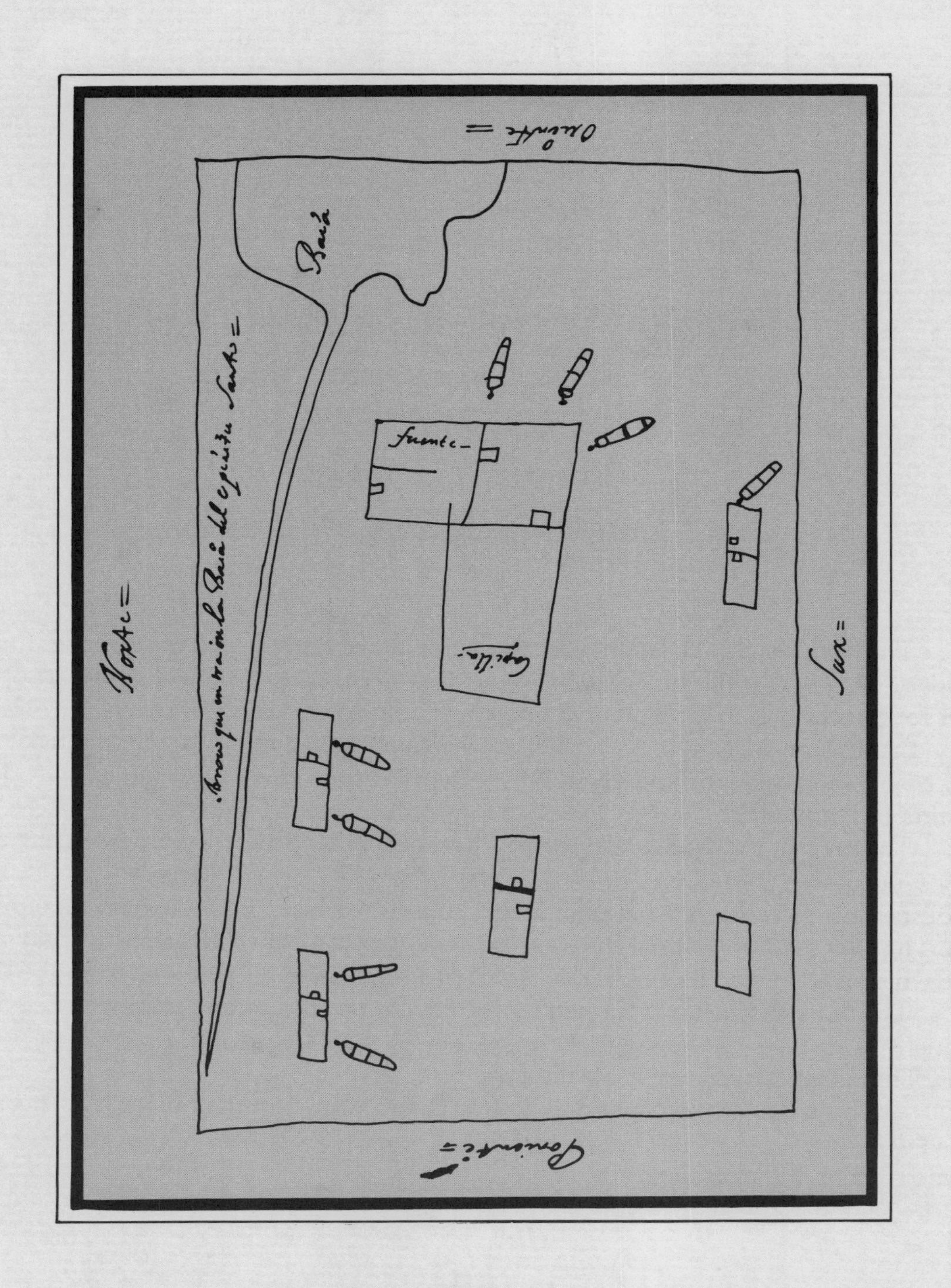
Norte=
Sur=
fuente

Presidio Nuestra Senora De Loreto
At La Bahia Del Espiritu Santo
In The
Province Of Texas
New Kingdom Of The Phillipines

The Marquis de San Miguel de Aguayo outlined and opened the trenches for the foundation. He gave the octagonal fortress four serpentine extensions instead of the other four bulwarks. (The octagonal fortress should have had eight bulwarks.) He did this so that the fortress might be protected whenever there might not be enough soldiers to garrison the place. Behind them he established four towers to better defend the curtains and bulwarks.

The present garrison at the fortress numbers ninety men. By orders of the King (may God protect him), it is located at the same place where Monsieur de La Salle established his fortress. It is on high level ground overlooking the entire surrounding area. The adjacent San Gabriel River is fifty varas distant from the fortress and 40 varas wide where it is crossed by the bridge which is a league and a half away from the bay.

The outer perimeter is formed by the covered walkway and its slope. The inner perimeter is formed by the moat lying in front of the bulwarks and serpentine extensions. The covered walkway is a pallisade.

The quarters of the captain and officers are located in the bulwarks. Those for the soldiers are on their respective curtains. Each has its corral. The storehouses are (located facing) the parade ground.

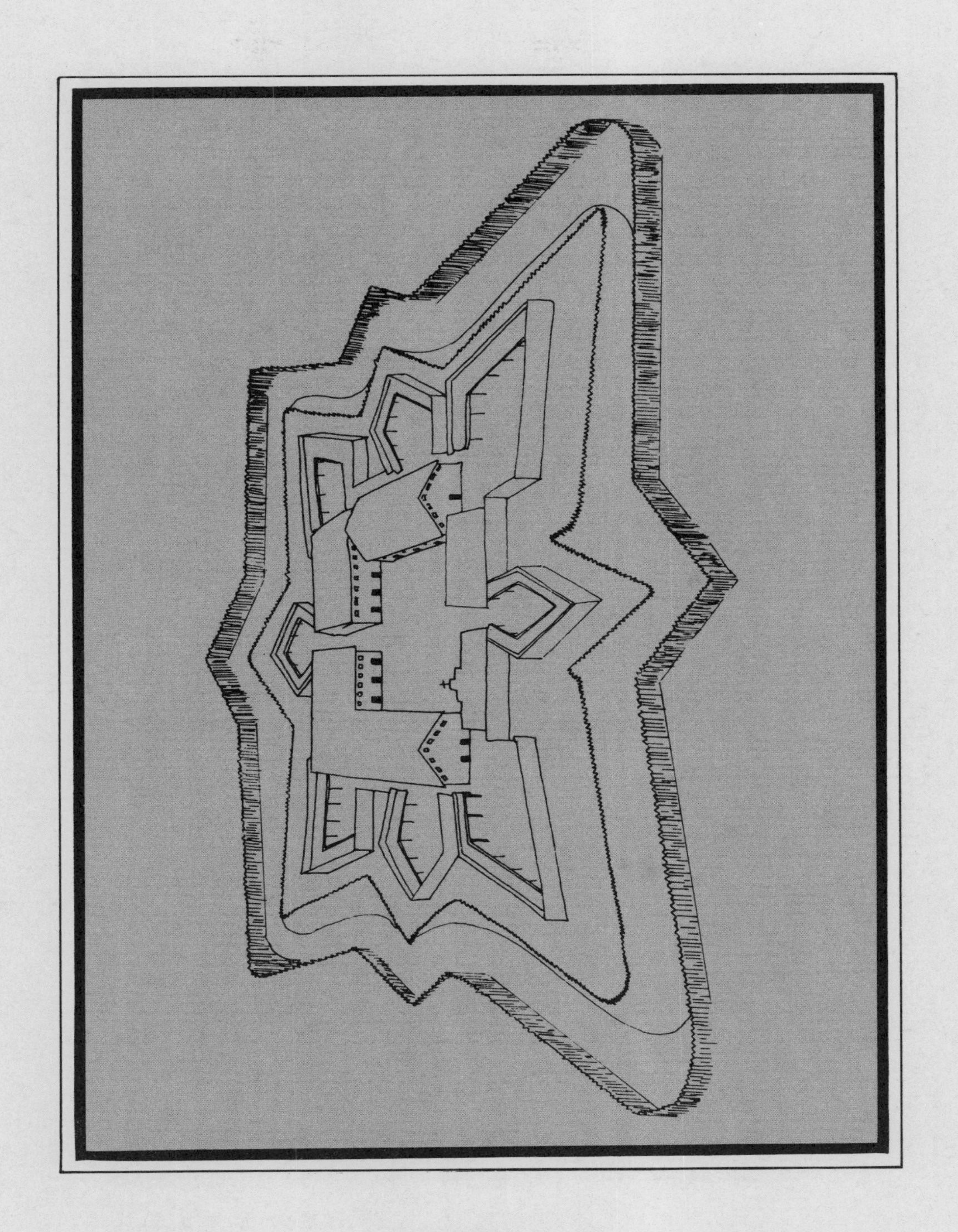

Presidio Nª. Sª. de Loreto
Río de San Gabriel
Espíritu Santo

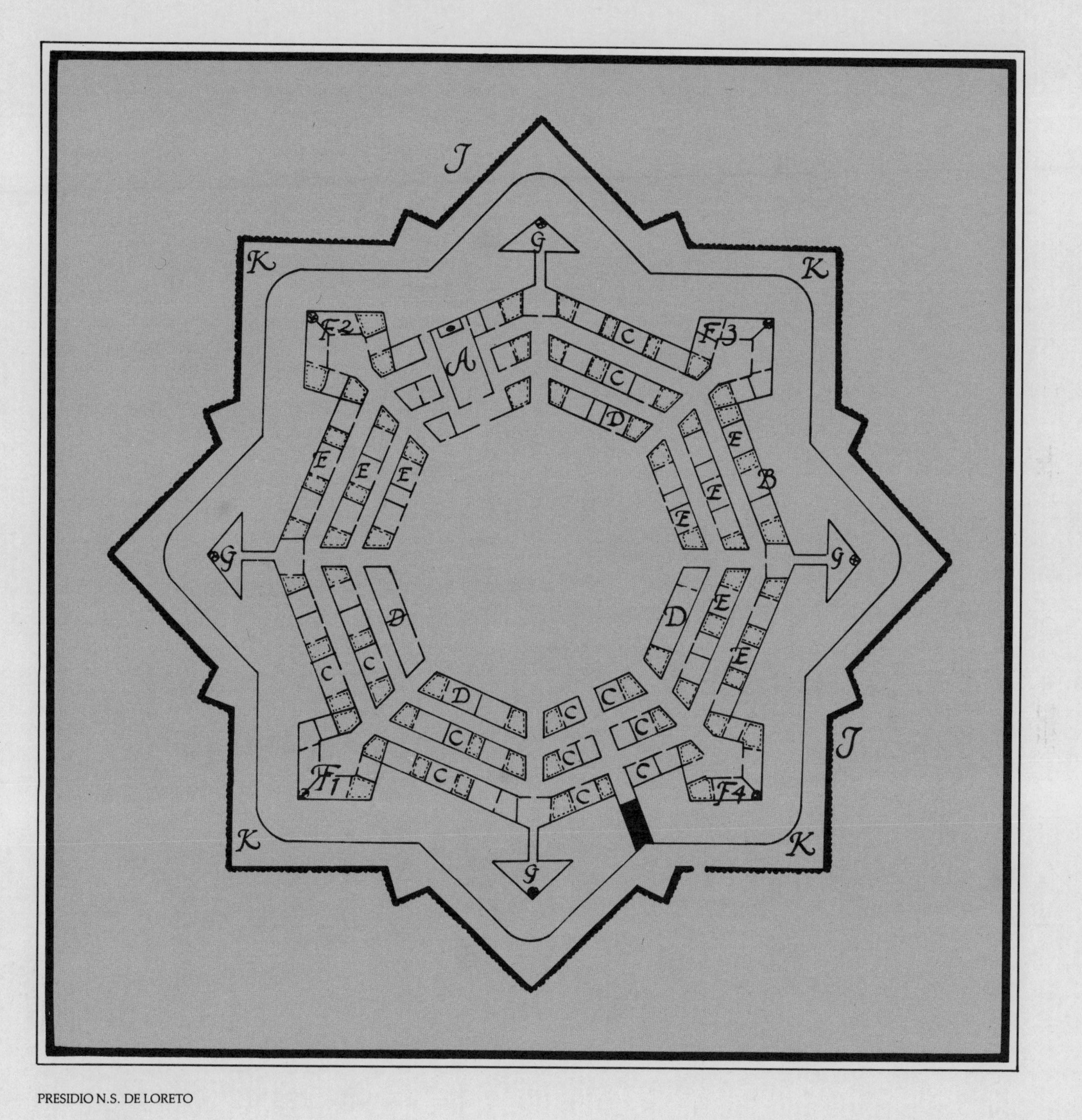

PRESIDIO N.S. DE LORETO

A. CHURCH
B. CURTAIN
C. OFFICER'S QUARTERS
D. STOREHOUSES
E. ENLISTED MEN'S QUARTERS AND CORRALS
F-1. BULWARK SAN RAFAEL
F-2. BULWARK ANGEL DE LA GUARDA
F-3. BULWARK SAN GABRIEL
F-4. BULWARK SAN MIGUEL
G. TOWERS
H. MOAT
I. SERPENTINE EXTENSIONS
J. PALLISADE
K. COVERED WALKWAY

Map Of The Bay Of Espiritu Santo In The Province Of The New Phillipines

The bay was observed by the Marquis de San Miguel de Aguayo on April 1, 1722. It was sounded with great care and precision. It is a beautiful port capable of embracing many ships in its 10 league canal which extends from Cape San Fernando to the sand-bar (at the mouth of the bay). The mouth is about 80 varas wide and over a league in length. (The canal) is 15 palms in depth.

The sand-bar adjacent to the mouth of the Guadalupe River is 11 varas deep and 10 varas wide. It is over a quarter league in length.

The sand-bar at the mouth of the San Gabriel is about 25 varas wide and a fourth of a league in length.

The flag was placed on high ground as a sign that the Presidio is located adjacent to the San Gabriel River. It is located beyond that point where launches cannot go.

The sweet-water springs are identified with a @. The two (springs) on cape Our Lady of Good Fortune are small and cannot support more than 25 soldiers.

The place where the fortress is to be erected will be the key to Espiritu Santo Bay. It is located at 28°23′.

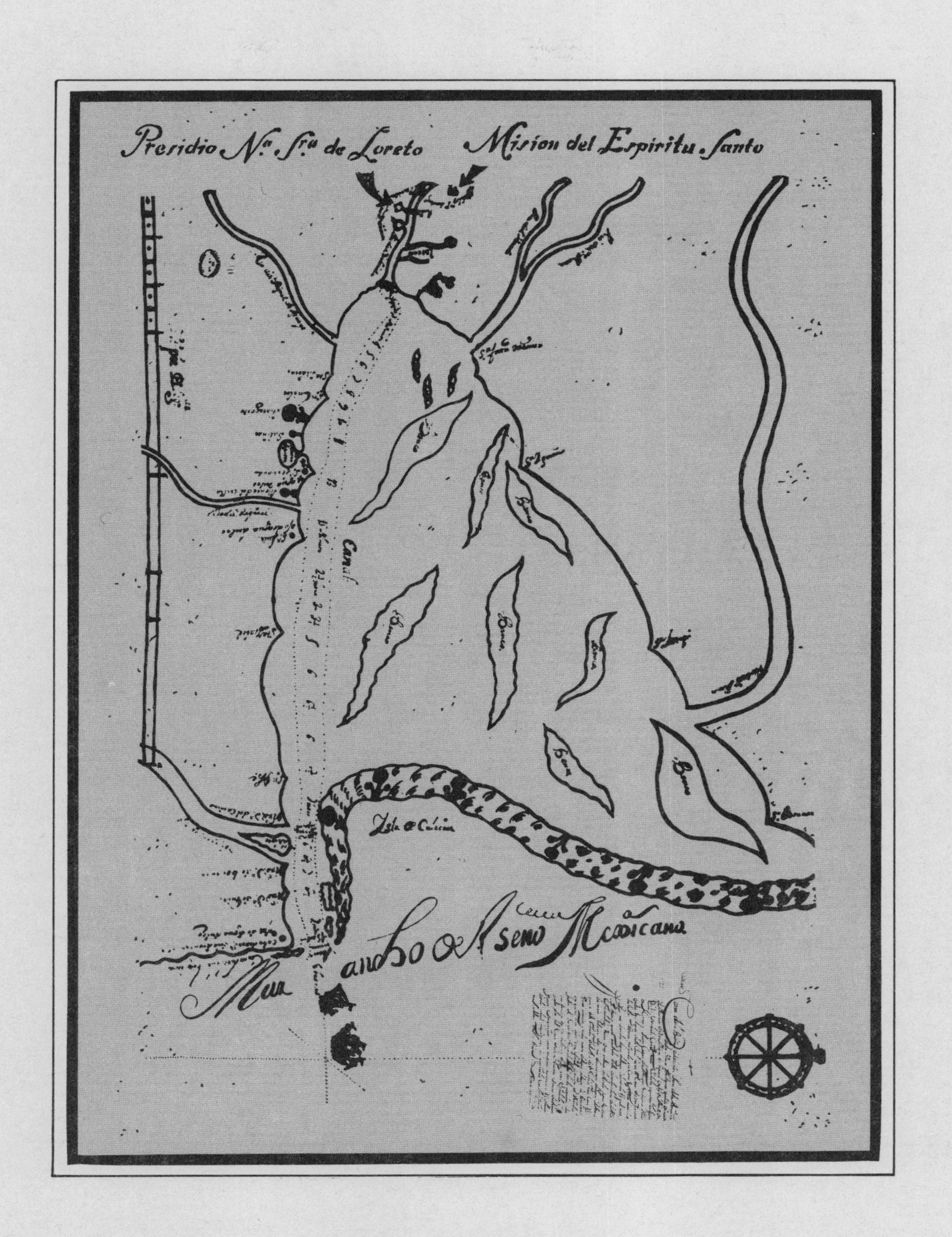
Presidio Nº. Srª de Loreto
Mision del Espiritu Santo
Canal
Mar ancho del seno Mexicana

Earliest Known Map Of San Antonio Area January 1722

This is a photocopy of the original, earliest known map of the San Antonio area done by, or for, the Second Marquiz de Aguayo in January 1722. The map, which has never been in any archival collection and bears no signatures, stamps or registry identification, is drawn on white linen, colonial map paper measuring 13 by 17 inches. A fine quill pen and liquid, black printers' type ink was used to draw the map.

There are some minute but substantial differences between this (the original map) and the copy on file in the Archivo General de la Nacion de Mexico. The one in Mexico City was copied by the same cartographer but drawn on colonial cotton paper.

The Second Marquiz de Aguayo was notorious for getting his directions mixed up. This would help explain why north is drawn pointing east on the map. Moreover, Fray Antonio Margil de Jesus, Fray Felix Isidro de Espinoza and diary keeper Fray Juan Antonio de la Pena would not have committed this error. Also note that the horse-shoe bend of the San Antonio River is depicted upside down.

The actual date upon which Aguayo recommended the founding of the City of San Antonio is not presently known. It is known, however, that the Spanish court approved the plan in 1723. It is also known that in January of 1722 Aguayo relocated the presidio to the site between the San Pedro Creek and the San Antonio River. It is also known that at that time Mission San Jose y San Miguel de Aguayo was still on the east bank of the river.

In March of 1722, Aguayo approved the establishment of Mission San Francisco Xavier de Najera to be located between missions San Antonio de Valero and San Jose. It is not known if any buildings were ever constructed at Mission de Najera though it is known that in 1726 the mission Indians were re-settled with the Indians at Valero.

It is also known that when Brigadier General Don Pedro de Rivera visited San Antonio in August of 1727, Mission San Jose was located on the west bank of the river.

In light of the foregoing annotations, it may be assumed that the map was drawn by, or for, the Second Marquiz de Aguayo in January 1722 upon his return to the Presidio de San Antonio from East Texas.

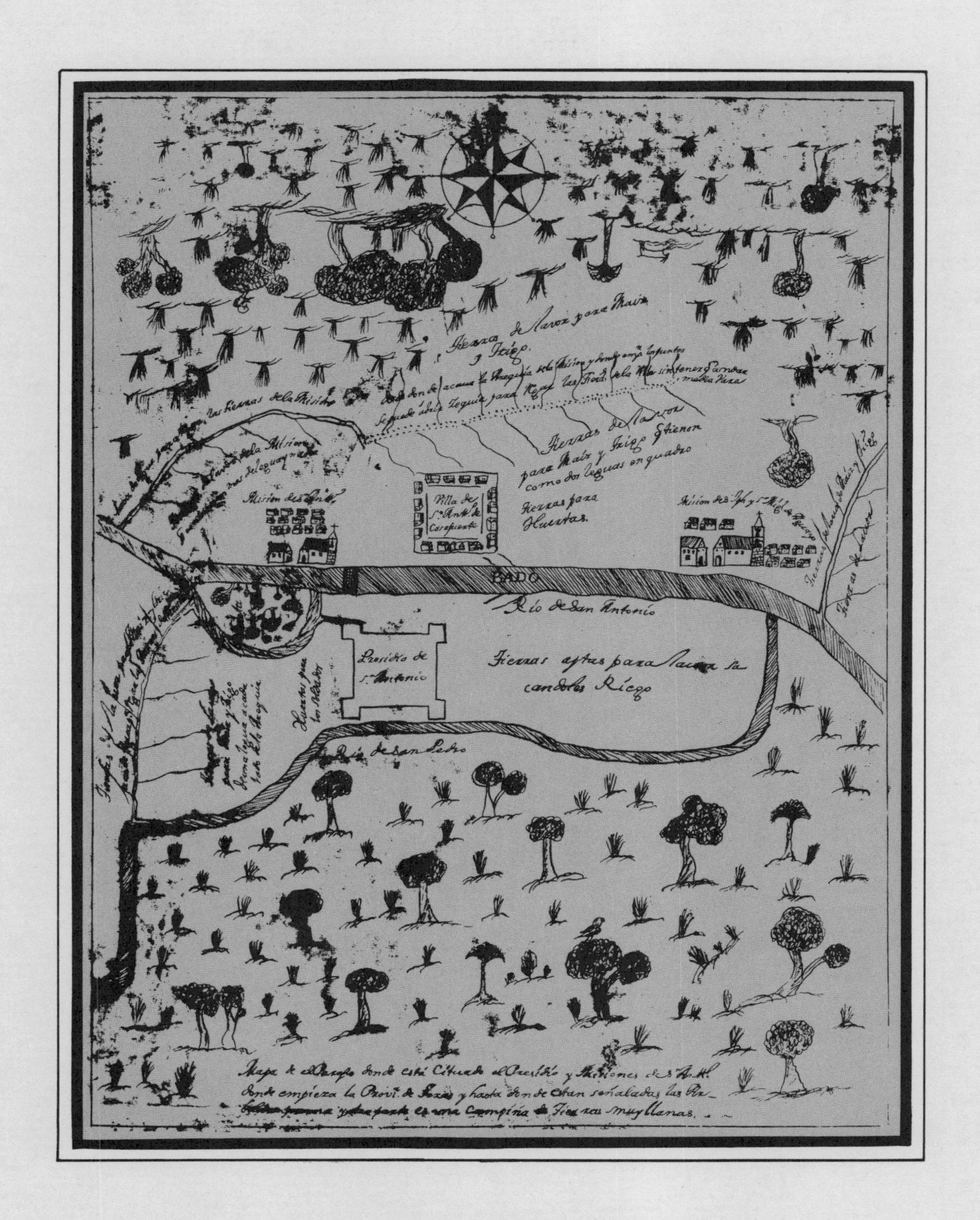
BADO
Rio de San Antonio
Presidio de S. Antonio
Rio de San Pedro
Tierras para Huertas
como dos leguas en quadro

Route Of The Aguayo Expedition

Plotting the route of the Aguayo expedition through Texas was no easy task. The first part of the journey, from the Rio Grande to San Antonio was fairly easy. Aguayo more or less followed the route established since 1709 by the Aguirre-Espinosa expedition. A number of times Aguayo struck a slightly different course, but it was always near the old, or known, road.

The second part of the journey, from San Antonio to Los Adaes, was very difficult. Aguayo chose a more northerly course than that used by previous expeditions. This could be blamed on cacique Juan Rodriguez who guided the expedition. It could also be blamed on Aguayo seeking to avoid as many waterways as possible.

The third part of the journey, from San Antonio to fort St. Louis on the Lavaca Bay, was not as difficult as expected. The greatest problem here was the unavailability of a certain topographical map. The map (U.S. Geological Survey, NH 14-9; Seguin) remains totally un-available at this time. This author-translator finally had to settle for the Texas General Highway county map series. These maps depict all roadways and waterways. Even though the maps are not topographical maps, they are still excellent for tracing colonial routes.

The diary itself (all five versions) presented three other problems in tracing the route of the expedition. First, the waterways in the formative years of Spanish Texas were known by different names to different people. Sometimes, the name of a certain waterway was given to another only because it lay in the same vicinity. Fr. Isidro Felix de Espinosa complained about this on June 23, 1716, when speaking of the San Juan and Trinity River. "The river of San Juan, sometimes mistaken for that of the Trinity, is not the same along this route we have just followed. . . . That is the reason why many who do not observe the route by which they enter or leave (the land of the) Texas cannot distinguish one from the other."

The second problem in following the route described in the diary was faced by the marchers themselves; the weather. The year 1721 was a wet one for Texas. The creeks and rivers were swollen or flooded. Creeks looked like rivers. Low water crossings looked like lagoons. Marshes and bayous looked like lakes. Moreover, one should remember that 250+ years ago there was a great deal more water in Texas than there is today. The water was not being used or wasted by a highly industrial population.

The third problem in following the route of the expedition as recorded in the diary lies in the various errors and differences of the five versions. Fortunately, Pedro de Rivera more or less followed the same route for the last fourth of the journey to Nacogdoches and Los Adaes in 1727. He also followed the same route from San Antonio to the Guadalupe River when going to Presidio Loreto and Mission Espiritu Santo. Had it not been for the Rivera Diary, this author-translator might still be trying to unravel Aguayo's erratic tramplings throughout east Texas and western Louisiana.

All waterways recorded by de la Pena and named by Aguayo are identified in the footnotes of this translation. However, the major waterways, Aguayo's names and their contemporary names are listed as follows:

PRESIDIO SAN JUAN BAUTISTA TO SAN ANTONIO

Rio Grande (Bravo del Norte)		Paso de Francia 100°18′W — 28°16N
Nueces River		approx. 2 miles upstream of Hwy 83 crossing, east of Crystal City
Leona River	Encinos del Rio Frio or Rio de los Muertos	at the Zavala-Frio county line
Frio River	Arroyo Hondo	approx. 8 miles northeast of the Missouri-Pacific railroad line
Hondo Creek	Charco de la Pita	FM 2200 and Hondo Creek
Medina River		IH 35 crossing

PRESIDIO SAN ANTONIO DE BEXAR TO NACOGDOCHES

Cibolo Creek		IH 35 crossing—Missouri Pacific Railroad
Guadalupe River	San Ybon	approx. 1 mile downstream of 377
San Marcos River	Rio de los Inocentes	downtown San Marcos, Texas
Blanco River	San Rafael	Missouri-Pacific Railroad crossing
Colorado River	San Marcos	Hwys 71, 183 crossing
Brushy Creek	San Xavier	Norman Crossing
San Gabriel	San Ygnacio	Hwy 97—Missouri-Kansas-Texas RR
Little River	Segundo Brazos de Dios	Missouri-Kansas-Texas RR. crossing (note three rivers mentioned by de la Pena as being directly north thus being the Salado Creek, Leon River and Lampasos River)

Bosque River	Jesus Nazareno	directly east of Bosqueville
Brazos River	Tercer Brazos de Dios	directly northeast of Waco at western edge of Steinbeck Bend
Little Brazos River	Real del Patrocino de N.S.	Southern Pacific RR crossing
Navasota River		near junction with Camp Crk. directly east of Camp Creek Lake
Trinity River		Hwy. 19—Missouri Pacific RR
Neches		Hwy 7-103
Angelina River	Santa Barbara	John Durst Crossing

N.S. GUADALUPE DE NACOGDOCHES TO LOS ADAES

Attoyac River	Todos Santos	Hwy. 21
Sabine River	San Francisco de las Sabinas	near junction with Grannies Creek in Shelby County
Presidio Los Adaes		see diary and footnotes

SAN ANTONIO DE BEXAR TO PRESIDIO LORETO

Salado Creek		Hwy 181
Cibolo Creek		FM 887
Ecleto Creek	Cleto	approx. 1 mile above its junction with San Antonio River
Guadalupe River		in vicinity of DeWitt-Victoria county line
Presidio N.S. de Loreto and Ft. St. Louis		see diary and footnotes

Red River
Sabine River
Attoyac Bayou
Neches River
Angelina River
Trinity River
Brazos River
Bosque River
Little River
San Gabriel River
Colorado River
Blanco River
Guadalupe River
Cibolo Creek
Leon Creek
Medina River
Leona River
Frio River
Nueces River
San Antonio River
Matagorda Bay

FOOTNOTES

1. *Su Señoría* (His Lordship) does not appear in version B.
2. Mobile, now State of Alabama, was founded by the French in 1698.
3. Penzacola, now State of Florida, was founded by the Spaniards in 1559.
4. *Se han* (they have) appears as *se ha* (it has) in versions B, C, D, and E.
5. The French settlement at Natchitoches dates from at least 1714 (exact date unknown because it was an Indian Village), but the French presidio was established in 1717.
6. *Rio de la Empalizada* was the Mississippi, not the Missouri. De la Peña erred. At one time it was also known as Espíritu Santo.
7. See footnote six (6).
8. *Los* (the) appears in versions A, D and E; but not in B or C.
9. *Día* (day) appears in versions A, D and E; but not in B or C.
10. *Fuerzas* (forces) appears in A and E; but not in B, C or D.
11. Versions A, D and E say *retirándose* (retreating) while versions B and C say *retardandose* (being delayed, retarded, slowed down).
12. The six Franciscan missions were: San Francisco de los Texas, Purísima Concepcíon, San Joseph de los Nazonis, Nuestra Señora de Guadalupe, Nuestra Señora de los Dolores, and San Miguel de los Adaes.
13. The Real Presidio and Villa de San Antonio de Bexar was founded by Governor Don Martín de Alarcón on May 1, 1718.

14. The reader should remember that during the Spanish-Mexican colonial period the boundary line between Coahuila and Texas was the San Antonio-Medina-Nueces rivers. That boundary line was no more than 12 miles from (now downtown) San Antonio.

15. *Compañía* (company) appears in versions A, D and E; but not in B or C.

16. The Reyno de Nuevo León (Kingdom of New León) was most instrumental and important in the exploration and settlement of Spanish Texas. Most of what is now Texas and Coahuila originally belonged to the Reyno de Nuevo León. The conquistadores and settlers of Nuevo León first colonized Coahuila and then moved on to Texas. See *Historia de Nuevo León* by Eugenio del Hoyo (Monterrey, 1972) which excels all other works on this topic.

17. Saltillo, Coahuila was founded in 1576 by Captain Alberto del Canto (see Eugenio de Hoyo, *Historia de Nuevo León*).

18. Parras, Coahuila founded circa 1578 (Eugenio de Hoyo, *ibid*).

19. *Mayor* (major) appears in A, D and E; but not in B or C.

20. Presidio San Francisco de Coahuila next to the town of Santiago de Monclova, was founded in 1674.

21. *Exitado* (excited) appears only in version C; the others read *explicado* (explained). This translator chose *excitado* (excited) because it makes more sense than the latter.

22. *Asunto* (matters) appears only in version C, all other verions read *aumento* (augmentation). This translator chose the former because it makes more sense than the latter.

23. Versions A, D and E read *establecer* (establish), while versions B and C read *erigir* (erect).

24. Versions A, D and E read *erigió* (erected), while versions B and C read *estableció* (established).

25. Versions A and E read *Joseph*, while B, C and D read *José*.

26. *Y para* (and *by*) appears in A, D and E, but not in B or C.

27. Versions A, D and E read 3,600 (horses) but verions B and C read 6,600.

28. *Y dejado* (and left) appears in versions A, D and E but not in B or C.

29. Versions A, D and E read *viniendo* (coming), while versions B and C read *llegando* (arriving).

30. Don Fernando Pérez de Almazán was a surveyor in 1714, at Saltillo working under Don Joseph de Azlor y Virto de Vera, second Marquis de San Miguel de Aguayo. In 1717, he surveyed some land recently acquired by the Marquis which had originally belonged to the conquistador Francisco de Urdinola. Obviously employed by the Marquis de Aguayo, he was the most logical choice for the position of Lieutenant-General of the expedition. As lieutenant-Governor, Don Fernando Pérez de Almazan is left in command of Texas when Aguayo returned to Coahuila. By recommendation of the Marquis, Pérez de Almazan is named Governor of Texas in 1722. He first established the capital at Los Adaes but was forced to remove himself to San Antonio in 1725. He resigned his position in 1727, and is said to have gone to Mexico City in 1729.

31. Nothing is presently known of Captain Thomas Zubiria other than that which appears in this diary. He was not with Ramón (1716) or Alarcón (1718). He was probably under the direct employ of the second Marquis de San Miguel de Aguayo.

32. Nothing is presently known of Captain Miguel Colón y Portugal before this expedition. He was not with Ramón (1716) or Alarcón (1718). He was probably in the employ of Aguayo for in 1741, he is still a Cavalry Captain and *Alcalde Mayor* at Saltillo. (See Vito Alesio Robles, *Coahuila y Tejas en la Epoca Colonial*; pp. 461-462).

33. Captain Don *Manuel* Gabriel Costales in versions B and C is identified as Gabriel Costales in A, D and E. He was not with Ramón (1716) or Alarcón (1718). He was also most likely under the employ of Aguayo.

34. Nothing is presently known of Captain Don Manuel Herrera other than that which appears in this diary. He was not with Ramón (1716) or Alarcón (1718). It is interesting to note that a *Diego Herrera* moved from Los Adaes to San Antonio in 1793.

35. Nothing is presently known of Captain Don Francisco Bezerra Luque other than that which appears in this diary. He was not with Ramón (1716) or Alarcón (1718).

36. Nothing is known of Captain Jose Arroyo other than that which appears in this diary. He was not with Ramón (1716) or Alarcón (1718).

37. Nothing is known of Captain Don Pedro de Uribe (or Oribe), other than that which appears in this diary. He too is not with Ramón (1716) or Alarcón (1718).

38. Nothing is known of Captain Don Juan Cantú other than that which appears in this diary. He too was not with Ramón (1716) or Alarcón (1718). It is interesting to note that the Cantú family of early Nuevo León and Coahuila was related to conquistador, Captain General Don Alonso de León and that the Cantús served under de León in his expedition to Texas in search of La Salle. (See Israel Cavazos, *Cedulario Autobiográfico de Pobladores y Conquistadores de Nuevo León* [Monterrey, 1964]).

39. Versions A, D and E read *ha de gobernar*, while versions B and C read *ha de manejar.*

40. Fight for your faith and King.

41. Saint James the Greater, patron saint of Spain. Versions A, D and E read *Patrón Santiago*, while versions B and C read *Padre y Señor Santiago.*

42. Word order in this phrase is reversed. Versions A, D and E read *Procession, Misa y Sermon*; while B and C read *misa y sermon y procesión.*

43. Versions A, D and E read *capitanes* (captains), while versions B and C read *oficiales.* The latter seemed more appropriate.

44. Versions A, D and E exclude *general*, but B and C include it when referring to Pérez de Almazán as the Lieutenant-General.

45. Versions A, B, D and E read November *16th* and only version C reads November *17th.*

46. Versions B and C exclude the word *creciente* (flood), but it appears in versions A, D and E.

47. Versions A, D and E read *se emplearon tres semanas* (three weeks were spent), while versions B and C read *se detuvieron . . . tres semanas* (for three weeks we were delayed).

48. Franciscan Friar Isidro Felix de Espinoza was born in Queretaro, Mexico on November 26, 1679. He entered the College of the Holy Cross of Querétaro on March 19, 1697, and was ordained one year later. In 1709, he was assigned to Mission San Juan Bautista del Rio Grande and in April of that same year he accompanied Captain Pedro de Aguirre in his expedition to East Texas. In 1715, he was named Pres-

ident of the Texas missions belonging to the College of the Holy Cross and the following year he accompanied Captain Domingo Ramón to East Texas. During this expedition he founded missions Purísima Concepción de los Hainai, San Francisco de los Texas, and San Joseph de los Nazonis. In 1718, he met Governor Martín de Alarcón at San Antonio and helped establish Mission San Antonio de Valero. He went to Mexico City in late 1718, and returned to Texas with Aguayo.

49. Vito Alesio Robles in *Coahuila y Tejas en la Epoca Colonial* (p. 474), says Dr. Don Joseph Codallos y Rabál was the assignee and administrator of the marquisate of San Miguel de Aguayo.

50. Versions A, B, D and E all read *delegación* (delegated powers) but version C reads *denegación* (denegation, refusal).

51. At this time Texas, Coahuila, Nuevo León, and most of the frontier still belonged to the bisphoric of Guadalajara.

52. Franciscan Mission San Bernardino de la Caldera was founded August, 1674.

53. Franciscan Mission Santiago de Valladares was also founded in 1674. By 1695 the Indians of this mission as well as those of San Bernardino had moved to San Pedro de Boca de Leones. Only ten families of Tlaxcaltecan Indians are said to have remained. On December 22, 1718, the land of San Bernardino de la Candela and Santiago de Valladares were surveyed and granted to the Indians. It is very possible that the Marquis de Aguayo did not visit these missions solely to distribute gifts as much as to help launch the Indian Pueblo.

54. The phrase *de el* (his, on his own, of it, . . .,) appears in version B, and as *del* in versions A, C, D and E. *On his own* was chosen in this translation because the Marquis de Aguayo did clothe the Indians at his own expense.

55. Franciscan Mission San Miguel de Luna (also called San Miguel de Aguayo) was founded in 1716.

56. Franciscan Mission San Buenaventura, 20 miles west of Monclova, was founded in 1673.

57. Versions A and D read *diferentes experiencias;* versions B and C read *varias experiencias;* and version E reads *diferentes modos.*

58. Versions A, B, D and E read *no se pasaron mas que seis;* but version C reads, *no se pasaron mas que dos, digo seis. . . .* This error lends weight to the theory that the known copies were written by scribes from a dictation.

59. Rev. Peter Forrestal (Peña's Diary of the Aguayo Expedition, p. 9) erred in translating *Nadadores* as swimmers. The indios Nadadores lived along the Rio de los Nadadores.

60. Versions A and E correctly read *indios sanas* but versions B, C and D read *indios samas.*

61. Louis Juchereau de St. Denis was born 1676, in Canada. He served on the Hudson Bay in 1698 and in France in 1699. In September 1699, he left France for Louisiana serving with Pierre le Moyne D'Iberville to explore the lower Mississippi River. In 1913, Louisiana Governor Antoine de la Mothe Cadillac sent St. Denis to San Juan Bautista del Rio Grande to negotiate commercial trade with the Spaniards. He arrived on July 18, 1714, and was sent to Mexico City by the Spanish commandant Diego Ramón. St. Denis returned the following year and married the commandant's granddaughter, Manuela Sánchez de Ramón. In 1716, he led the Ramón expedition into Texas and thence went on to Mobile. St. Denis returned to San Juan Bautista in 1717, and was arrested by the Spaniards. He was imprisoned in Mexico City and released on November 22 on his own recognizance. St. Denis escaped and managed to return to Natchitoches. His activities for 1721-1722 are reported in this diary. Louis de St. Denis died on June 11, 1744.

62. Versions A and E read *recibió* (received) but versions B, C, and D read *resolvió* (resolved).

63. The marginal numbers appear in versions A, D and E, but not in B or C.

64. Nothing is known of this officer other than that which appears in this diary. He was not with Ramon (1716) or Alarcón (1718).

65. On August 15, 1722, the Marquis de Aguayo left Captain Juan Cortinas in charge of the presidio Nuestra Señora de los Dolores (see diary). A certain Juan Cortinas, son of Juan Cortinas received land in San Antonio on October 24, 1743. The Juan who received the land had been a member of the militia and ad-interim captain of the Presidio San Juan Bautista del Rio Grande. He could have been the same Juan Cortinas who came to Texas with the Aguayo expedition.

66. Franciscan Friar Benito Sánchez had come to Texas in 1716 with the Ramón Expedition. He had been assigned to Mission San José de los Nazonis by Friar Isidro Felix de Espinosa. Friar Sanchez obviously retreated all the way to Mission San Juan Bautista del Rio Grande when the French invaded Texas.

67. Mission San Juan Bautista was founded on June 22, 1699, along the Rio Sabinas. It was moved January 1, 1700 to the vicinity of present day Guerrero, Coahuila on the road to *Nueva Francia y los Tejas.*

68. Presidio San Juan Bautista del Rio Grande was founded in 1703. Before then, it had been a military outpost commanded by Captain Diego Ramón.

69. Fr. de la Peña begins the diary at the Paso de Francia on the Rio Grande. It is located at 100°18′W, 28°16′N (U.S. Geological Survey Map, NH 14-10; Eagle Pass).

70. Only version C does not include the word *real* (camp, place, site). It appears on all other versions.

71. Campsite *real del Cuervo* was well known and used by practically all Spanish and Mexican expeditions entering Texas from San Juan Bautista. Aguayo's campsite was apparently located on the eastern branch of the Cuervo Creek where it crosses FM 1021. See U.S. Geological Survey Map HN 14-10; Eagle Pass.

72. Fr. de la Peña apparently erred in identifying this site as Rosas de San Juan. The given direction and length of march would place the expedition at San Ambrosio Creek some two (2) miles south of where its eastern branch crosses FM 2644. Both the San Ambrosio and Rosita(s) de San Juan were well known and used by the Spanish and Mexican expeditions. In light of the descriptions and length and march cited for the following days, however, it becomes obvious that de la Peña confused the San Ambrosio for Rositas de San Juan. See U.S. Geological Survey Map, NH 14-10; Eagle Pass.

73. Ojo (spring) de San Diego was apparently located on the western, un-named extremities of Carrizo Creek at approximately one (1) mile west of Fed 277, and two (2) miles south of Rocky Creek (where it crosses Fed 277). See U.S. Geological Survey Map, NH 14-11; Crystal City.

74. Carmanchel is apparently present-day Turkey Creek. The campsite must have been located two (2) miles due east of S.H. 83. See U.S. Geological Survey Map, NH 14-11; Crystal City.

75. The archaic *guexolotes* and *guejolotes* used in the versions of the diary for the contemporary *guajolote* (turkey). The fowl is referred to as being the peacock of the indies *(pavo de las indias).*

76. This entry for Saturday, March 29, does not appear in versions B or C!

77. The expedition apparently marched north-northeast along the Turkey (Caramanchel) Creek thence turned easterly to cross the Nueces at approximately two (2) miles upstream from where S.H. 83 crosses the river. See U.S. Geological Survey Map, 14-11; Crystal City.

78. This dry creek is probably the eastern branch of Turkey Creek at approximately one (1) mile upstream from where S.H. 83 crosses the creek. See U.S. Geological Survey Map, NH 14-11; Crystal City.

79. This crossing and campsite was apparently located immediately below the junction of Torgua Creek and East Branch Tortuga Creek. See U.S. Geological Survey Map NH 14-11; Crystal City.

80. Encinos del Rio Frio is presently known as the Leona River. This campsite was apparently located on the upper branches of the Leona alongside FM 117 in the vicinity of the *Old Woodward Ranch.* See U.S. Geological Survey Map NH 14-11; Crystal City.

81. River of the Dead.

82. Versions A, D, and E read *flores* (flowers) while versions B and C read *rosas* (roses).

83. Traveling east-southeast along the Leona River we encounter a low water crossing where the Zavala and Frio County lines cross the river. See U.S. Geological Survey Map, NH 14-11; Crystal City.

84. Campsite los Gatos would be located on the upper branch of present day Live Oak Creek in the vicinity of the Loxton Ranch. See U.S. Geological Survey Map, NH 14-11; Crystal City.

85. This un-named *dry ravine* (which is still un-named) lies directly west of the Rio Frio which de la Peña called Arroyo Hondo. Later travelers in apparent confusion gave the same name to a nearby creek still known as the Hondo Creek.

86. The Arroyo Hondo of de la Peña is the present-day Frio River. It was crossed approximately eight (8) miles northeast of the Missouri-Pacific Railroad tracks (which lie on the western edge of Pearsall) and directly east of the first curve on F.M. 140. See U.S. Geological Survey Map, NH 14-11; Crystal City.

87. *Y el arroyo* (and the creek) appears in versions A, D and E, but not in versions B or C.

88. Campsite and creek called Tulillo is presently called Seco Creek. The campsite and crossing was at approximately two (2) miles downstream from where the creek crosses the Medina-Frio county lines. See U.S. Geological Survey Map, NH 14-8; San Antonio.

89. De la Peña's *Las Cruzes* is apparently one of the nameless branches of the Hondo Creek.

90. This entire passage does not appear in versions B or C.

91. *Charco de la Pita* is presently known as the Hondo Creek. This campsite and crossing was located at the intersection of FM 2200 and the creek. See U.S. Geological Survey Map, NH 14-8; San Antonio.

92. The Medina River was apparently crossed where the Missouri Pacific Railroad track crosses the river directly north of I.H. 35, S.H. 81. See U.S. Geological Survey Map, NH 14-8; San Antonio.

93. Does not appear in B or C.

94. The Medina-San Antonio river boundary between Texas and Coahuila did not change until after 1836.

95. The Leon Creek was crossed in the vicinity of the U.S.H. 81 and the Missouri Pacific Railroad tracks.

96. The villa (town) and Real Presidio San Antonio de Bexar was founded by Governor Martín de Alarcón on May 5, 1718. Alarcón surveyed all the land from the headsprings of the San Antonio River to where the San Pedro Creek enters the river. He could not find a suitable site for the villa and presidio. On May 5, he finally established the presidio but did not record the actual site. He did say that Mission San Antonio de Valero was located *three-quarters of a league* down the creek. Historians have been arguing and debating the site of the villa, presidio and mission ever since.

97. Franciscan Mission San Antonio de Valero was founded by Governor Martín de Alarcón and Fr. Antonio Olivares de San Buenaventura on May 1, 1718. Like the presidio and villa, the original first site of Mission de Valero (the Alamo) is unknown.

98. Te Deum Ladamus (we praise you God), a Roman Catholic hymn.

99. Blessed are they who come in the name of God.

100. Antonio Margil de Jesús was born in Valencia, Spain on August 18, 1657. He entered the Franciscan Order on April 22, 1673. He was assigned to Mexico and arrived at Vera Cruz on June 6, 1683. Fr. Margil de Jesús was stationed at the College of Holy Cross of Querétaro and was thence sent to Guatemala. On June 25, 1706, he was appointed the first Guardian of the College of Guadalupe de Zacatecas. He came to Texas with the Ramón expedition of 1716 and founded three missions in east Texas (Dolores de los Ais, San Miguel de los Adaes, and Guadalupe de Nacogdoches). Fr. Margil retreated to San Antonio de Bexar when the French invaded and there received Aguayo's approval to establish Mission San José y San Miguel de Aguayo in 1719.

101. Friar Gabriel de Vergara is listed in versions A and E, but not in versions B, C, or D. He had first come to Texas in 1716, with the Ramon expedition.

102. Friar Joseph Guerra is listed in versions A and E but not in versions B, C or D. Nothing is presently known of this missionary than that which appears in this diary.

103. Nothing is presently known of this missionary other than that which appears in this diary. There is a Fr. Joseph (Antonio) Rodríguez who in the 1730's became very active in the missions along the Rio Grande.

104. Fr. Joseph's last name is given as *Albadadejo* in versions A, D and E, but as *Abadadejo* in B and *Abadejo* in C. Nothing is known of this missionary other than that which appears in this diary.

105. Nothing is known of Br. Joseph Pita. In 1724, however, Aguayo reported Br. Pita had been killed by the Apaches. See *Autos sobre diferentes puntos consultados por el Gobernador* de la provincia de Texas, 1724.

106. *Fija* (firm) appears in versions A, D and E but not in B or C.

107. Versions A and E read *Santo Zelo* (holy zeal), versions B and C read *Su Señoría* (His Lordship) and version E reads *su santo* (his saint, holy).

108. Versions A, D and E read *marcha* (march, field) while versions B and C read *armas* (arms, service, field).

109. Versions A, D and E read *muchas misiones* (many sermons, praying sessions); but versions B and C read *muchos misioneros* (many missionaries).

110. The salt beds referred to here must have been either La Sal del Rey in present Hidalgo County or La Sal Vieja in Willacy County. It is important to note that armed men from Nuevo León were coming to the site since before 1721.

111. Versions A, D and E read *que allí habitan* (who live there), while B and C read *que allí habitaban* (who lived there).

112. His complete name was Joseph Domingo Ramón. He was the son of Captain Diego Ramón (I). Joseph or José Domingo Ramón was a brother-in-law of Louis de St. Denis who had married the daughter of Diego Ramón (II). The Ramón family had served with distinction on the military outposts of Coahuila

and Don Diego (I) had succeeded Alonso de León to the Governorship of Coahuila in 1691. His ad-interim office ended in 1693, and Don Diego returned to military service on the frontier. He had been encharge of the military outpost of San Juan Bautista in 1701, and became its first captain when it became a presidio in 1703. His sons Diego (II), Joseph Domingo, and Andres also served at San Juan Bautista. Joseph Domingo Ramón was chosen by his father to head the 1716 expedition to east Texas with Fr. Isidro Felix de Espinosa. In 1719, he was forced to retreat to San Juan Bautista. He returned to Texas with Aguayo. José Domingo Ramón's activites in this expedition can be followed in this diary. He died at La Bahía on December 23, 1723, and succeeded by his son Diego Ramón III.

113. El dia dies de marzo (on the tenth of March) appears in versions A, D and E but not in B or C.

114. The reader should not confuse this Bahía del Espíritu for the later mission by that name. In fact, this reference is to the *bay* of Espíritu Santo now known as Lavaca Bay site of La Salle's Fort St. Louis.

115. In light of this information, it can be ascertained that Joseph Domingo Ramón arrived at the bay on April 11. On the 13, he dispatched the four Indians to San Antonio who arrived on the 18. It had taken Ramón and company two days to sound out the bay!

116. *Expuestos* (likely) appears only in versions B and C.

117. *Un día* (a day) does not appear in B or C.

118. De Valero does not appear in B or C.

119. The reader should keep in mind that there is a distinct difference between the *Province of the Texas Indians and the land of the Texas.* Rev. Forrestal erred in translating and understanding this passage by saying (p. 19, ft. 21) that ". . . Texas comprised only the territory between the Trinity and Red Rivers and part of what is now Louisiana."

120. The water from the San Antonio River was drawn from a well-known site in what is now Brackenridge Park in the vicinity of the Witte Museum.

121. Una legua (a league) does not appear in B or C.

122. This crossing and campsite is located approximately where U.S.H. 81 crosses the Salado Creek. See U.S. Geological Survey Map, NH 14-8; San Antonio.

123. Una legua (a league) appears only in A and E, and not in B, C and D.

124. Todo género (all types) does not appear in versions B or C.

125. This crossing and campsite is located approximately where the Missouri-Kansas-Texas Railroad tracks cross the Cibolo Creek. See U.S. Geological Survey Map, NH 14-8; San Antonio.

126. Versions A and E read *nornordeste* (north-northeast) while versions B, C and D read nordeste (northeast). Mathematically, the route figures out to be north-northeast.

127. This entire passage does not appear in versions B, C or D.

128. This creek and campsite should be the Dry Comal Creek at FM 1863. See U.S. Geological Survey Map, NH 14-8; San Antonio.

129. De la Peña apparently confused the Blieders Creek for the Guadalupe River. It could not have been the Guadalupe because he placed the San Ybon River as being "at about three-quarters of a league" ahead. Mathematically, as well as by description, de la Peña's Guadalupe is the present-day Blieders Creek and de la Peña's San Ybon is the present day Guadalupe. See U.S. Geological Survey Map, NH / 14-8; San Antonio.

130. Versions A, D and E read *mas bajo* (lowest, more low) while versions B and C read *mas braveo* (more rapid, more fierce).

131. ferns.

132. Muy (very) does not appear in versions B or C.

133. De la Peña's San Ybon is the present day Guadalupe River. See footnote 129 above.

134. Muchas (many) does not appear in versions B or C.

135. Campsite and Arroyo Panuelas is present day York Creek at either the Missouri Pacific or Missouri-Kansas-Texas railroad crossings. See U.S. Geological Survey Map, NH 14-8; San Antonio.

136. *Con mesquital* (with mesquite) does not appear in versions B or C.

137. *Grande* (large, grand, great, vast) does not appear in versions B or C.

138. Rio de los Innocentes is the present day Comal. Pedro de Rivera's entry for August 21, 1727, verifies this.

139. *Dos* (two, or in this case, *both*) does not appear in versions B or C.

140. This author-translator has been unable to trace the origin and true meaning of this archaic idiomatic expression.

141. *Muy* (very) does not appear in versions B or C.

142. *Mas abunda* (most abounding, most abundant) does not appear in versions B or C.

143. *La presta* (the pledge) does not appear in versions B or C.

144. The San Rafael Creek is the present day Blanco River. See diary of Pedro de Rivera (entry for August 21, 1727) for verification. Rivera wrote: ". . . the arroyo San Rafael which others call the Blanco."

145. Versions A, D and E read *despachó* (dispatched, set out) while versions B and C read *mandado* (ordered, sent out).

146. *No* (not, in this case) does not appear in versions B or C.

147. Versions A and E read *nornordeste* (north-northeast) while versions B and C and D read *nordest* (north-east).

148. *Demas* (the rest) does not appear in version B.

149. *Muy* (very) does not appear in versions B or C.

150. Campsite and Arroyo San Bernardino is located on Slaughter Creek where U.S. 81 (IH 35) cross it. See U.S. Geological Survey Map, NH 14-6; Austin.

151. Rio Las Garrapatas is one of the extremities of present day Onion Creek at approximately one mile north of Bluff Springs. See U.S. Geological Survey Map, NH 14-6; Austin.

152. Both Forrestal (p. 23, ft. 24) and buckley (Aguayo Expedition, Quarterly, XV, p. 38, ft. 2) identify this as McKinny Falls on Onion Creek.

153. De la Peña's San Marcos River is the present day Colorado River. According to the diary's descriptions and mathematical computations it was crossed where U.S. 181 and S.H. 71 both cross the river. See U.S. Geological Survey Map, NH 14-6; Austin.

154. Versions A, D and E read *por uno y otro costado,* while versions B and C read *por uno y otro lado.* Although both phrases carry the same meaning, it is interesting to note the differences in phraseology.

155. The contemporary creek which exists at this point is not named in the topographical map (U.S. Geological Survey Map, NH 14-6; Austin).

156. This author-translator was unable to derive the true meaning of this colorful but archaic idiomatic expression. It is obvious, however, that de la Peña was not particularly pleased or impressed with the buffalo's appearance.

157. The reader should remember the Spaniards were using a different system of reading latitude and longitude (Theide Peak of Tenerife instead of Greenwich). Therefore, there is an approximate 25 to 30 minute difference in Spanish colonial and contemporary readings. This will be discussed in the chapter concerning the route of the Aguayo Expedition.

158. *Profundo* (deep) does not appear in versions B or C.

159. De la Peña's San Francisco Creek is the present day Left Walnut Creek in the vicinity of where it is crossed by I. H. 35. See U.S. Geological Survey Map, NH 14-6; Austin.

160. Versions A, D and E read 50 soldiers but versions B and C read 54.

161. *Casi* (almost) does not appear in versions B or C.

162. De la Peña's Arroyo Las Animas is the present day Gilleland Creek at approximately one mile northeast of Three Points. Buckley (op.cit.) claimed it was the Brushy Creek, but that is mathematically impossible. See U.S. Geological Survey Map, NH 14-6; Austin.

163. One of the many un-named creeks and ravines directly south of the Brushy Creek.

164. De la Peña's San Xavier River is the present day Brushy Creek. It was crossed in the vicinity of the Norman Crossing which is located just about at 30°30′ Latitude and 97°30′ Longitude. See U.S. Geological Survey Map, NH 14-6; Austin.

165. Another of the un-named creeks and ravines directly south of Brushy Creek.

166. De la Peña's San Ignacio River is the present day San Gabriel which was crossed approximately where it is crossed by S. H. 97 and the Missouri-Kansas-Texas Railroad tracks. The topography immediately south of the river indicates the presence of a creek now long dried. The creek mentioned by de la Pena as being on the opposite (north) side is the present day Queen branch. See U.S. Geological Survey Map NH 14-6; Austin.

167. This entire passage does not appear in versions B or C.

168. Versions A and E read *nornordeste* (north-northeast) but versions B, C and D read nordeste (northeast). Mathematically, however, the route figures out north-northeast along the route of S.H. 97 and the Missouri-Kansas-Texas Railroad track.

169. De la Peña's San Fernando Creek is the present day Indian Creek north of Bartlett, Texas where it is crossed by US 97 and the Missouri-Kansas-Texas Railroad track. See U.S. Geological Survey Map, NH 14-6; Austin.

170. This passage by de la Peña is not clear. Did he (as Buckley assumed) refer to passing 20 creeks on this one day? Or, was he counting major creeks from San Antonio? The latter seems more plausible.

171. This nameless creek is the present day South Darrs Creek, directly west of where it is crossed by the Missouri-Kansas-Texas Railroad line. See U.S. Geological Survey Map, NH 14-6; Austin.

172. De la Peña's Espíritu Santo Creek is the present day Willow Creek which runs in the old river bed of the Little River. Therefore, it is entirely possible that when Aguayo's Expedition reached this point in 1721, they actually crossed the Little River before it changed its course along the bed. The exact location (figured mathematically) is on the Willow Creek where it is crossed by the Missouri-Kansas-Texas Railroad line directly south of Sparks.

173. This is the first mention of the families which went along with the expedition to settle in East Texas. Most, if not all of these families, were forced to move to San Antonio in 1793.

174. The old road crossing referred to is where the Pacific Railroad and S.H. 79 cross the Brazos River. This crossing later used by Pedro Rivera and others, is below its junction with the Little River, Brushy Creek and all other creeks passed by the Aguayo Expedition. See U.S. Geological Survey Map, NH 14-6; Austin.

175. Version A reads *otros* dias (other days), versions B, C, and D read *los tres dias* (the three days), and version E crossed out the number and appears as *los otros dos dias* (the other two days).

176. The author-translator's identification of the Little River or Willow Creek as de la Peña's Espiritu Santo Creek is verified by the identification of these three creeks. They are, the Lampasos River, Leon River, and Salado Creek. They come together in the triangle formed by Sommers Mill, Port Griffin and Wilson Valley. See U.S. Geological Survey Map, NH 14-6; Austin.

177. This first tributary mentioned by de la Peña should be on the site of the present day Little River or on its bed.

178. This second tributary appears on the topographical map but its name is not given. See U.S. Geological Survey Map, NH 14-3; Waco.

179. *Mucho* mas (*very* much) does not appear in versions B or C.

180. Even though this creek appears on the topographical map, its name does not. See U.S. Geological Survey Map, NH 14-3; Waco.

181. *Aquella noche* (i.e. the night before) does not appear in versions B or C.

182. Versions A, D and E read nornordeste (north-northeast) while versions B and C read nordeste (northeast).

183. Like the other creeks in this area, this one too is shown on the map even though its name is not given. This one, however, is directly west of Heidenheimer between highways 95 and 36. See U.S. Geological Survey Map, NH 14-3; Waco.

184. De la Peña's San Norberto Creek is the present day Knob Creek. The crossing and campsite is where the creek is crossed by S.H. 36 and the Gulf-Colorado and Santa Fe Railroad line. See U.S. Geological Survey Map, NH 14-3; Waco.

185. Versions A, D and E read *nornordeste* (north-northeast) but versions B and C read *nordeste* (northeast).

186. The hills and creeks mentioned by de la Peña are east of present day Temple, Texas.

187. De la Peña's San Antonio de Padua Creek is the present day Cottonwood Creek where it is crossed by IH 35, U.S. 81, and the Missouri-Kansas-Texas Railroad lines. See U.S. Geological Survey Map, NH 14-3; Waco.

188. Version C (only) reads *tres veces* (three times).

189. De la Peña's San Joseph de los Apaches is the present day un-named creek (an upper tributary of Deer Creek) at approximately Eddy, Texas on IH 35, U.S. 81, and the Missouri-Kansas-Texas Railroad line. See U.S. Geological Survey Map, NH 14-3; Waco.

190. It is a well known fact that the buffalo was never domesticated because it could not be kept in captivity. After being roped, buffalos would die or kill themselves. It is obvious, however, that the members of the Aguayo Expedition did not intend to domesticate these buffalos.

191. The Spaniards in the colonial period took their readings from Theide Peak on the Island of Tenerife (one of the Canary Islands). In contemporary Greenwich readings it would be 31°17N-97°15W.

192. De la Peña's San Joachin y Santa Ana is impossible to locate today due to the construction of Lake Waco.

193. *Considerable* (considerable) does not appear in versions B or C.

194. De la Peña's Rio Jesus Nazareno is the present day Bosque River immediately northwest of Waco, Texas. It was crossed directly east of Bosqueville.

195. The third branch of the Brazos referred to by de la Peña is the present day Brazos River directly northwest of Waco, Texas. The Bosque and Brazos rivers were apparently crossed at their nearest point on the western end of Steinbeck Bend. See U.S. Geological Survey Map, NH 14-3; Waco.

196. *Muy* (very) appears only in B and C.

197. *Altos* (tall) does not appear in versions B or C.

198. It appears that Steinbeck Bend along the junction of the Brazos and Bosque rivers directly northwest of Waco was a pond or lagoon in 1721.

199. De la Peña's San Sylverio Papa is the present day Tehuacana Creek about two (2) miles south of its junction with Roberts Creek. See U.S. Geological Survey Map, NH 14-3; Waco.

200. Version A reads *sueste* (southeast), versions B and C read *Lueste* (southeast) but versions D and E read *Lesueste* (east-southeast). However, the same sentence then says they turned southeast. Therefore, the first reading should be east-southeast as recorded in D and E.

201. De la Peña's San Jorge Creek is the Manos Creek at S.H. 6 some two (2) miles northwest of Riesel, Texas. See U.S. Geological Survey Map, NH 14-3; Waco.

202. east.

203. De la Peña's San Juan de los Jumanos is the present day Big Sandy Creek directly north of where it enters the Marlin City Lake. See U.S. Geological Survey Map, NH 14-3; Waco.

204. Versions A, D and E read *facilitar el transito* (to facilitate the crossing) but versions B and C read *para pasar* (to cross).

205. De la Peña's Real del Patrocino de Nuestra Señora is the present day Little Brazos River where it is crossed by the Southern Pacific Railroad line between Bremond and Reagan, Texas. See U.S. Geological Survey Map, NH 14-3; Waco.

206. This is either the Big Willow or the Walnut Creek between S.H. 6 and Nesbitto, Texas. See U.S. Geological Survey Map, NH 14-3; Waco.

207. De la Peña's Angel de la Guarda Creek is the South Walnut Creek on the second road which crosses it southwest of Owensville on the road to Calvert. See U.S. Geological Survey Map, NH 14-3; Waco.

208. De la Peña's Nuestra Senora del Camino is today directly east of Calvert, Texas about four (4) miles west of U.S. 79. See U.S. Geological Survey Map, NH 14-3; Austin.

209. De la Pena's Nuestra Señora de Guia is the un-named creek one mile directly northeast of Franklin, Texas on U.S. 79 and Missouri Pacific Railroad line. See U.S. Geological Survey Map, NH 14-3; Waco.

210. This reading is totally unreconcilable not only with contemporary readings, but with previous readings as well! One can only assume that whoever took the reading erred tremendously.

211. San Pedro y San Pablo is in Camp Creek Lake or its vicinity. See U.S. Geological Survey Map, NH 14-3; Waco.

212. This passage is an obvious reference to Camp Creek and the Navasota River directly east of Camp Creek Lake. See U.S. Geological Survey Map, NH 14-3; Waco.

213. Nuestra Señora de la Estrella is on the east bank of the Navasota River in Madison County directly south of West Caney Creek. See U.S. Geological Survey Map, NH 14-6; Austin.

214. The creek over which a bridge had to be built was the Sheppard Creek at approximately where it is crossed by S.H. 21. The marsh to the right was the Navasota River.

215. Campsite Real de la Visitacion de Nuestra Señora was along the eastern branch of the Gibbons Creek at exactly 96° longitude. See U.S. Geological Survey Map, NH 14-6; Austin.

216. Arroyo San Buenaventura and Real de la Visitacion were one and the same place. See footnote 215 for the location.

217. The manuscripts (all of them) actually read *tigre* (tiger) but it must have been a reference to either mountain lions or bob-cats.

218. It seems as if the area directly northeast of Roans Prairie, Texas must have been part of the lake or lagoon mentioned in the diary. The area in question is found between the triangle formed by S.H. 90, S.H. 30, and the Fort Worth and Denver-Chicago-Rock Island and Pacific Railroad lines.

219. Little if anything is known of this relief column of 1719.

220. The small creek identified by de la Peña as Nuestra Señora del Rosario is one of the nameless branches of the South Bedias Creek. Its location is approximately 2 miles west of the Walker-Grimes county line, and approximately ten miles south of the Madison-Grimes county line. See U.S. Geological Survey Map, NH 15-4; Beaumont.

221. De la Peña's Carrizo Creek is the present day Rocky Creek due west of Huntsville, Texas. See U.S. Geological Survey Map, NH 15-4; Beaumont.

222. De la Peña's Santa Clara Creek, also known as Las Cruces, is the present day Parker Creek due north of Huntsville, Texas at about 30°45'N. See U.S. Geological Survey Map, NH 15-4; Beaumont.

223. This creek in question was the Harmon Creek directly east of Huntsville, Texas near the church located along its western bank. See U.S. Geological Survey Map, NH 15-4; Beaumont.

224. The reader should bear in mind (as related in the diary's next passage) that the Aguayo expedition went off course in order to visit the Indian Rancherías. Compare this route to that of Pedro de Rivera who

said the Santa Clara was only eight (8) leagues away from the Trinity. In light of the distances and descriptions given, Arroyo de Nuestra Senõra del Buen Suceso can be triangulated as being the East Fork of the San Jacinto River in the vicinity of the Walker-San Jacinto county line. See U.S. Geological Survey Map, NH 15-4; Beaumont.

225. De la Peña obviously misspelled or hispanicized *fleur de lis.*

226. De la Peña's Arroyo Santa Rosa is the present day nameless creek which enters the Trinity River right at the San Jacinto-Walker county line. See U.S. Geological Survey Map, NH 15-4; Beaumont.

227. Aguayo apparently reached the Trinity River where it is now crossed by both S.H. 19 and the Missouri-Pacific Railroad line. See U.S. Geological Survey Map, NH 15-4; Beaumont.

228. Versions A, D and E read *creciente* (flood) while versions B and C read *corriente* (speed, rapids).

229. Versions A, D and E read *habiendo sido la detencion para todo esto* (Our total delay for all this was) while versions B and C read *haviendo sido la demora* (the delay having been of).

230. Nicolas de los Santos Coy came to Texas in 1716 with Ramon.

231. De la Peña's Arroyo San Juan is the present day nameless creek on the north bank of the Trinity directly east of S.H. 19 and the Missouri-Pacific Railroad line. See U.S. Geological Survey Map, NH 15-4; Beaumont.

232. Versions A, D and E read three and a half varas while versions B and C read three varas.

233. Versions A, D and E read *aynay* but versions B and C read *Adais.*

234. This entire phrase does not appear in version C.

235. *Santa* (Holy) does not appear in versions B or C.

236. De la Peña's Santa Efigenia Creek is the present day Dads Creek at approximately 31°00'N-95°16'W. See U.S. Geological Survey Map, NH 15-4; Beaumont.

237. The marginal notation of total leagues marched in not included in versions A or E.

238. De la Peña's Santa Coleta is the present day Piney Creek where it crosses the Houston-Trinity county line. See U.S. Geological Survey Map, NH 15-1; Palestine.

239. De la Peña's San Pedro is in the vicinity of the North Fork Cedar Creek directly south of the Houston-Travis county line. It is imperative to note that de la Peña said this was the site of the first (Texas) Presidio. See U.S. Geological Survey Map, NH 15-1; Palestine.

240. Versions A, D and E read *los indios, e indias, con sus criaturas de los ranchos,* while versions B and C read *las indias con sus criaturas y los indios de los ranchos.*

241. Versions A and E read *elotes* (corn) while versions B, C and D read *flores* (flowers).

242. parched corn, ground and mixed with sugar and water.

243. Versions A, D and E read *señor gobernador,* but versions B and C read *su señoria* (His Lordship).

244. This site is later identified as being on the west side of the Angelina River along S.H. 21 in the vicinity of Allen Creek. See diary entries for August 6th, 7th and 8th. Also see U.S. Geological Survey Map, NH 15-1; Palestine.

245. According to this description, the 1716 presidio would be located in the square formed by S.H. 7 on the north, Pine Island on the east, Cochino Bayou on the south (which de la Peña apparently called a lagoon), and the old Logging Railroad Line. The site is almost at 95°00′ W. See U.S. Geological Survey Map, NH 15-1; Palestine. The campsite on the Neches must have been where S.H. 7 meets the west bank of the river.

246. The Nacono, Nacona, Nacomone Indians belonged to the Caddoan tribe and lived primarily in what is now Nacogdoches County.

247. Versions A, D and E read *elotes* (corn) while versions B and C read *flores* (flowers).

248. Vayeta (bayeta . . . flannel) does not appear in versions B or C.

249. Rev. Forrestal excluded this item in his translation. Quezquemiles (also quesquemiles and/or Quexquemil) is a hood worn by Indian maidens. See Francisco J. Santamaria, *Diccionario de Mejicanismos* (Porrua, 1959; Mexico).

250. This entire phrase does not appear in versions B, C or D.

251. "French" is excluded from versions B and C.

252. The French presidio among the Cadadoches would be the one established in 1700 near the mouth of the Mississippi River. De la Peña later describes it as being sixty leagues from Natchotoches.

253. Louís de St. Denis was actually correct in describing the site unsuitable. Aguayo had to move the mission further away from the river for its banks kept flooding the old (1716) site. See this diary for elaboration.

254. Versions B and C read *Padre Presidente y Fr. Joseph Guerra* (the father president *and* Friar Joseph Guerra). The missionary president during this expedition was Fr. Isidro Felix de Espinosa.

255. *De los Religiosos* (of the religious) does not appear in versions B or C.

256. *Desde San Antonio* (since San Antonio) does not appear in versions B or C.

257. *Ganado* (cattle) does not appear in versions B, C or D.

258. This description places the second site of the 1716 presidio as being east of the Neches River in the triangle formed by S.H. 7, S.H. 103 and Bodan Creek. See U.S. Geological Survey Map, NH 15-1; Palestine.

259. De Jesus appears only in versions B and C.

260. Versions A, D and E read 158 but versions B and C read 188.

261. *Y muchachos* (and children) does not appear in versions B or C.

262. *Y deseo* (and desire) does not appear in versions B or C.

263. Versions A, D and E read *hasta cerca* (almost) while versions B and C read *mas* (over, more than).

264. The march for this day might have started east-northeast, but it apparently ended going practically north and slightly northwest. Creek and Campsite Nuestra Señora de las Nieves is the present day unnamed creek four (4) miles northwest of Wells on U.S.H. 69. See U.S. Geological Survey Map, NH 15-1; Palestine.

265. Versions A and E read *rio pequeño* (small river), versions B and C read *otro arroyo* (another creek), and version D reads *arroyo pequeño* (small creek).

266. Rev. Forrestal translated this passage as "small permanent creek." However, it is imperative to note de la Peña's effort to point out that the creek is permanent and that it has water year round.

267. *Su senoría* (His Lordship) does not appear in versions B or C.

268. De la Peña's Santa Barbara is the present day Angelina River at the John Durst Crossing. R. B. Blake did a remarkably good job in 1938 in identifying this site (Quarterly, XLI, pp. 212-224; "Locations of the Early Spanish Missions and Presidio in Nacogdoches County"). This author's computations and Blake's research both agree that Mission Concepcion was located on the east bank of the Angelina River. The presidio was located about a mile east. See U.S. Geological Survey Map, NH 15-1; Palestine.

269. Versions A, D and E read *su Señoria* (His Lordship) while versions B and C read *señor Gobernador* (Governor).

270. Versions A, D and E read *destruida* (destroyed).

271. Version B reads *tres* (three) but it was crossed out and *diez* (ten) was written over it. Version C reads *tres* (three). Versions A, D and E all read *diez* (ten).

272. This entire phrase does not appear in versions B or C.

273. This entire phrase does not appear in versions B or C.

274. Versions A and E read *mision* (mission). Version D reads *mansion* (abode), and versions B and C exclude both words.

275. This phrase does not appear in versions B or C. However, there is an illegible correction or notation at this place in version B.

276. Versions A and E read *elotes* (corn). Versions B and C read *flores* (flowers). Version D reads *flotes* (an obvious spelling error).

277. *Niños* (children) does not appear in versions B or C.

278. Even though mileage is given for this day, it is imperative to note that Aguayo and de la Peña did not go to San José de los Nazonis. Instead, it was Fr. Sánchez and a detachment.

279. This author-translator's mathematical computations and R. E. Blake's research agree on the location of Mission San José de los Nazonis as being in the vicinity of the tower directly northwest of Cushing, west of Elm Creek and directly south of the Nacogdoches-Rusk county line. See U.S. Geological Survey Map, NH 15-1; Palestine.

280. There is no question of Mission Nuestra Señora de Guadalupe de los Nacogdoches as being in Nacogdoches, Texas.

281. Only version C does not have *todos* (all).

282. Only version C spells it *Atinais.*

283. *Lesnas* (awls) does not appear in versions A, D and E.

284. Velduques (large knives [machete-type?] does not appear in versions A, D and E.

285. Even though eslabon can be a chain-link (as translated by Rev. Forrestal), the second definition (steel for striking flint) seems most appropriate.

286. *Chochomites* is probably a misspelling of the earlier *quezquemites.* They were the Indian hoods worn by the maidens.

287. This phrase does not appear in versions B or C.

288. *Entero* (complete) does not appear in versions A and E.

289. Versions A and E read *elotes* (corn). Versions B and D read *flotes* (obviously a writing error); and version C reads *flores* (flowers).

290. De la Peña's Arroyo de la Assumpcion is the present day Bayou Loco. The campsite and crossing was where the John Durst Road crosses the creek. See U.S. Geological Survey Map, NH 15-1; Palestine.

291. For the exact location of this mission, see R. E. Blake "Location of the Early Missions and Presidio in Nacogdoches County" (Quarterly, XLI, pp. 212-224).

292. *Cantada* (sung, or in this case High Mass) does not appear in versions B or C.

293. Versions A and E read *tres* (three) while versions B, C and D read *entre* (between).

294. Versions A, D and E read *gobernador* (governor) while B and C read *su Señoria* (His Lordship).

295. Versions A, D and E read que *se congregaran* (to congregate) while versions B and C read *que se juntaran* a pueblo (for them to form a township).

296. The direction of march for this day (even though all five versions agree) must be an error. Pedro de Rivera, who followed the same route just six years later, recorded that the road from Nacogdoches to Dolores was lest-Sueste (east-southeast). See Rivera's entry for Sept. 10, 1727. In light of this information and correction, we can then identify de la Peña's San Bernardo Creek as Moss Creek in the vicinity of S.H. 21. See U.S. Geological Survey Map, NH 15-1; Palestine.

297. Only version C includes this common phrase in reference to Fr. Margil.

298. *Destacamento* (detachment) does not appear in versions B or C.

299. Versions A and E read *un rio* (a river). Versions B and C read *un arroyo or rio grande* (a creek or large river). Version D reads *un arroyo, digo rio* (a creek, I mean a river). Actually, the expedition crossed both a creek and a river. See footnote number 300.

300. There are two mistakes in this entry which are repeated in all five versions. The first error is the direction of march. The direction was east-northeast. The second error was the given distance to the Todos Santos River, the present Attoyac River. This river was crossed where S.H. 21 crosses it today. See U.S. Geological Survey Map, NH 15-1; Palestine.

301. San Agustín, Texas.

302. Versions B and C include the word *reverendo* (reverend).

303. This distance measures perfectly back to the Attoyac River.

304. This entire phrase does not appear in versions B or C.

305. Versions A, D and E read east with variances to the east-northeast. Versions B and C read east with varances to the northeast.

306. Version C reads *paso* (passed, crossed).

307. De la Peña's laguna San Bartholome (and Rivera's Patron) is the present day Patroon Bayou. The Aguayo expedition camped on its west bank in the vicinity of Sexton, Texas and S.H. 87. See U.S. Geological Survey Map, NH 15-2; Alexandria.

308. Birthday of the Prince of Asturias.

309. Express sent from San Antonio on April 26.

310. *Muy espezas* (heavy) does not appear in versions B or C.

311. Version C reads *paso* (passed, crossed).

312. De la Peña's Laguna San Luis is the present day Grannies Creek directly east of Huxley, Texas. See U.S. Geological Survey Map, NH 15-2; Alexandria.

313. The Sabine River (San Francisco de Sabinas) was crossed by the Aguayo expedition immediate to its junction with Grannie Creek. Six years later, Pedro de Rivera crossed the river at the same place. See U.S. Geological Survey Map, NH 15-2; Alexandria.

314. Versions A and E read *coraza* (breast-plate). Versions B, C and D read *carroza* (coach).

315. De la Peña's San Tolentino is the present day extremity of McDonald Bayou about one mile east of La. Hwy. 174. See U.S. Geological Survey Map, NH 15-2; Alexandria.

316. *Su Señoria* (His Lordship) does not appear in versions B or C.

317. De la Peña's laguna Santa Rosa de Lima (and Rivera's San Miguel) is the present day Bayou San Patricio. The bayou was crossed in the vicinity of the Sabine-De Soto Parish line. The camp must have been near Pelican. (De Soto Parish) Louisiana. See U.S. Geological Survey Map, NH 15-2; Alexandria.

318. On September 14, 1727, Brig. General Pedro de Rivera marched fairly much along the same route from the Sabine to Pelican, Louisiana. He wrote: "On the fourteenth (I marched) towards the east a quarter northeast over land not much different from the day before. After crossing the (Sabine) river, I marched eight leagues and made camp at a clearing which lies between a creek called the San Miguel and the Caballada campsite." (The reader should remember that Rivera's San Miguel is the present day Bayou San Patricio.)

319. Versions B, C and D read *por el rumbo dicho* (in the given direction). Versions A and E read *Lesnordeste* (east-northeast). However, the actual directions of march (as verified by Rivera) was east-southeast! See Rivera's entry for September 15, 1727.

320. Only versions A and E do not include this passage.

321. Versions B, C and D do not include this passage.

322. De la Peña's campsite San Agustín is 4 miles northwest of Fort Jessup and six (6) miles northeast of Many, Louisiana. The creek referred to would be Harpoon Bayou on the west and Bayou Dupont to the northeast. See U.S. Geological Survey Map, NH 15-2; Alexandria.

323. *Mas adelante* (further on) does not appear in versions B or C.

324. This description would place the Presidio of Los Adaes and Mission San Miguel de los Adaes about one (1) mile southwest of Shamrock in the vicinity of the Sabine, Natchitoches Parish line. See U.S. Geological Survey Map, NH 15-2; Alexandria.

325. *Luego* (immediately) does not appear in versions B or C.

326. Version C reads six leagues.

327. It is interesting to note that Nicholas de la Fora gave the location of Los Adaes as 32°15'N-285°52'W. Pedro de Rivera gave it as 30°20'N-285°15'W.

328. *Muy devoto* (very devout) does not appear in versions B or C.

329. *Y a los capitanes* (and the captains) does not appear in versions B or C.

330. *Fiestas* does not appear in versions B or C.

331. *Encamisada* (masquerade) does not appear in versions B or C.

332. Versions A, D and E read *señor Gobernador* (Governor) and versions B and C read *Su Señoria* (His Lordship).

333. This entire passage took a great deal of computations and analysis to decipher but in doing so, it verified this author's placement and identification of the Presidio de los Adaes. First, los Adaes was seven leagues from Natchitoches. Second, a lake in between forced a ten league detour from Adaes to Natchitoches. Third, the road to Natchitoches was reached by crossing the Cadadoches River. The problem with all this (besides the fact that all this was ignored by other historians) is that there is presently no lake between Adaes and Natchitoches! There are however, a series of bayous along highway 6 northeast of Fort Jesup, all around Robeline, and south, east and northeast of Shamrock, Louisiana. It is entirely possible that due to the heavy rains encountered by Aguayo in 1721, the bayous had risen forming what seemed like a lake to de la Peña. If this was true, then the ten league detour would have been south to Fort Jesup then northeast to Old River about a mile south of highway 6. This detour measures 10 leagues! See U.S. Geological Survey Map, NH 15-2; Alexandria.

334. Versions B and C read *el señor Gobernador* (His Lordship dispatched) while versions A, D and E read *despacho su señoria correo* (His Lordship dispatched an express).

335. November 1, 1721.

336. *Presidio* was not in versions B or C.

337. *Y guarnecida* (and garrisoned) does not appear in versions B or C.

338. Version C reads *5*.

339. This description places the Presidio de Texas along the west bank of the Yellow Bank Creek along the John Durst Road. See U.S. Geological Survey Map, NH 15-1; Palestine. R. E. Blake (op. cit) identified the site as being on the same road but west of Legg Creek. It is entirely possible that the presidio was moved after 1721 and before 1793.

340. *Grande* does not appear in versions B or C.

341. This should be the same San Juan Creek identified enroute to east Texas. According to both de la Peña and Pedro de Rivera, the San Juan (Evangelista) Creek is directly east of the Trinity River along highway 19.

342. Probably the Big Sandy Creek at U.S. 290.

343. *En San Antonio* does not appear in versions B or C.

344. *Penalidad* (troublesome) does not appear in version C.

345. *Su Señoria* (His Lordship) does not appear in versions B or C.

346. The age old argument as to the location of the presidio is not solved by de la Peña's statement that Aguayo selected a *better site*. The most likely location for the 1721 presidio (before being moved) is on the west bank of the San Antonio River along Josephine St.

347. This is the site of present day City Hall. In fact, the so-called "Governor's Palace" sits on the west side of the presidio and it might be true that it was the commandancia or commander's quarters. However, there is no proof that the actual presidio building was ever completed.

348. Versions A and E read *fortificacion* (fortification). Versions B and C read *fundacion* (foundation, ground-work). Version D reads *formacion* (formation)!

349. The reader should remember that the 1718 and 1721 sites of Valero (Alamo) and San Jose are not known. There are several accounts by various historians as to their locations. However, there is still no definite proof of anything other than the fact that the missions were moved about. At this time, it is highly possible that Valero was located on the east bank of the San Antonio River in the vicinity of Josephine St. San Jose, according to Rivera's map, was located in the vicinity of Mission Concepcion.

350. Mission San Francisco Xavier de Najera was probably located at the present site of Valero (the Alamo). The mission Indians were incorporated with those of Valero in 1726.

351. Versions B and C give his name Joaquin Codallos.

352. Versions A and E list him as Cilón y Portugal. Versions B and C list him as Zilon y Gavilán. Verson E lists him as Zilon y Portugal. See footnote 32 concerning Miguel Colon y Portugal.

353. The Salado Creek was crossed at the Old Corpus Christi Road crossing south of Brooks A.F.B. See U.S. Geological Survey Map, NH 14-8: San Antonio.

354. The entire entry for Tuesday, March 17, does not appear in versions B, C and D.

355. De la Peña's Aguila Creek is the present day Eagle Creek. It was crossed at HWY 187. See U.S. Geological Survey Map, NH 14-8; San Antonio.

356. The Cibolo Creek was crossed at FM 887 in Karnes County. See General Highway Map, Karnes County; Texas Highway Dept.

357. Versions B and C do not include the entry for Thursday, March 19. There is an entry by that date in the manuscripts, but the content is that of March 20.

358. The crossing and campsite called Cleto by de la Peña is the present day Ecleto Creek directly west of Runge at 97°45′W.

359. Versions B and C include this entry as Thursday, March 20.

360. De la Peña's San Joaquin is the present day Yates Creek at FM 1020 in Karnes County. See U.S. Geological Survey Map NH 14-12; Beeville.

361. De la Peña's San Benito Creek lies directly north of Yorktown (DeWitt County) at 29°00′N and directly east of S.H. 119. See U.S. Geological Survey Map, NH 14-12; Beeville.

362. The Guadalupe River was crossed in the vicinity of the DeWitt-Victoria county lines. See U.S. Geological Survey Map, NH 14-12; Beeville.

363. Versions A, D and E read *les-sueste* (east-southeast) while versions B and C read en *el mismo rumbo* (in the same direction).

364. De la Peña's San Joseph is the present day Garcita's Creek at the first low water crossing below its junction with Willow Creek northeast of Victoria.

365. Going by de la Peña's given distances and direction, we reach the west bank of the Lavaca River at 28°45'N. This site is on an elevation, approximately four miles south of the Missouri Pacific Railroad crossing, and in the midst of a present day oil refinery. The 1722 (de la Peña?) map of Espiritu Santo (Lavaca) Bay supports the identification of this site. The map can be read clockwise beginning at the base, Cabo San Fernando (Cavallo Pass). Going north along the right we encounter Matagorda Island. Present day Espiritu Santo Bay and San Antonio Bay appear on the map as being the mouth of the Guadalupe River. Still going north along the coast we come to San Joseph (Powderhouse Lake). Farther north is Santa Isabel (Indian Point). Thence comes San Luis (Galliniper Point). Rio San Rafael (?) is the present day Chocolate Bay and Chocolate Bayou. Slightly north of this is San Fernando (Noble Point in the vicinity of S.H. 35 Causeway). The next identifiable point is Rio San Miguel de Aguayo (Placedo Creek). Present day Garcitas Cove and Venado Creek appear as small indentations on the map. Rio de San Gabriel with the presidio Loreto on the west bank and Mission Espiritu Santo on the east appear on top of the map. This is the present day Lavaca River. Please note the two small creeks on the east bank of the river. This should be Redfish Lake and the small body of water directly south of it. To the right (east) of the San Gabriel (Lavaca) river is a nameless creek with two small bodies of water. This should be Kellar's Creek with Huisache Cove and Kellar Bay. The major waterway to the right with two branches should be the Carancahua Creek (east and west branches) joining together to form a wide opened waterway (Carancahua Bay). The next identifiable major waterway lies far to the right (east). This should be the Colorado River. Running across the bottom is the Matagorda Peninsula.

    In light of all this information we can assume that the site called Presidio Loreto by de la Peña in the diary was on the west bank of the Lavaca River as reported above. The chosen site of Mission Espiritu Santo was on the east side of the river in the vicinity of the railroad junction about one mile west of Lolita. The reader should bear in mind, however, that the presidio was apparently never built! Aguayo chose the site and opened the trenches for the foundation, but there is no record of its construction or even if it existed at the same site! The Presidio and Mission were moved to the west bank of the Guadalupe River in 1726. Pedro de Rivera visited this site in 1727. Archeological excavations and research on all these sites might unravel the site or sites of Ft. St. Louis, Presidio Loreto, and Espiritu Santo. See U.S. Geological Survey Map, NH 14-12; Beeville. Also see plots of Fort St. Louis (1689) and Espiritu Santo (Lavaca) Bay (1722).

366. Fort St. Louis actually existed from 1685 to 1689. LaSalle had set sail in 1684, and the ruins of the fort were found by Alonso de Leon on April 22, 1689.

367. This entire passage does not appear in versions B, C or D.

368. *Flores* (flowers) appears only in versions B and C.

369. This entire passage does not appear in versions B or C.

370. Versions B and C read *20,000*.

371. Versions A, D, AND E read *señor virey* (Viceroy), while versions B and C read *Su Excellencia* (His Excellency).

372. Alarcon's Presidio de Bexar was a collection of huts which burned in 1721.

373. Versions A and C are printed copies of the diary and thus carry no signatures. Version E is a hand-written copy of version A. Versions B and D are faulty copies of another (unidentified) manuscript. Therefore, none of the five known versions of the diary carry the signature of de la Peña.

374. See the above for comments concerning signatures on the manuscripts. Versions A, B, and E give Fr. Codallos y Rabal's first name as *Joseph*. Version C gives it as *Jose*, and version D gives it as *Josse*. None of the signatures are authentic. Version D at the Mexican National Archives has an attached document styled an extract of the Aguayo diary but in reality it is nothing more than an incomplete summary of the de la Peña diary.

Bibliography

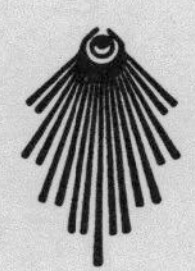

Peña, Juan Antonio de la *Derrotero de la Expedicion en la Provincia de los Texas que de orden del Exc. mo Señor Marques de Valero, Virey y Capitán General de esta Nueva España passa a executar el Muy Illustre Señor D. Joseph de Azlor, Caballero Mesnadero del Reyno de Aragon, Marques de S. Miguel de Aguayo, Governador y Capitán General de dichas Provincias de Texas, Nuevas Philipinas, y de esta de Coaguila, Nuevo Reyno de Estremadura.* [en la imprenta nueva plantiniana de Juan Francisco de Ortega Bonilla, en la calle de Tacuba (Mexico) 1722].

Peña, Juan Antonio de la "Diario del Viaje del Marques de San Miguel de Aguayo," Archivo General de la Nación de Mexico, Ramo de Historia, Vol. 28, expidiente num. 1; pp. 3r-63v.

Peña, Juan Antonio de la "Derrotero seguido por el Marques de San Miguel de Aguayo en su viage y expedición a la Provincia de Texas [1720-1722] para recuperarla de los invasores franceses de la Movila, reintegrar sus misiones y establecer barrera con la construcción de presidios en los Adays, Texas y Bahia del Espiritu Santo," *Documentos para la Historia Eclesiastica y Civíl de la Provincia de Texas o Nuevas Philipinas; 1720-1779.* [Ed. Porrua Turanzas, Madrid; 1961.]

Peña, Juan Antonio de la "Diario del Marques de San Miguel de Aguayo" Bibliotech Nacional de Mexico, Departamento de Manuscritos, Manuscritos de los Conventos, Legajo Num. 94, expidiente num. 2.

Peña, Juan Antonio de "Derrotero de la Expedición en la Provincia de los Texas, Nuevo Reyno de Philipinas que orden del Exc. mo. Sr. Marques de Valero, Virey y Capitán General de esta Nueva España, pasa a executar el Muy Ilustre Señor D. Joseph de Azlor, Cavallero Mesnadero del Reyno de Aragon, Marques de San Miguel de Aguayo, Governador y Capitán General de dichas Provincias de Texas, Nuevas Philipinas y esta de Coaguila, Nuevo Reyno de Estremadura." Archivo General de la Nación de Mexico, Ramo de Historia, vol. 302, expidiente num. 6, pp. 1r-52v.

Rivera, Pedro de *Diario y Derrotero de lo caminado, visto y obcervado en el discurso de la visita general de precidios, situados en las provincias ynternas de Nueva Espana* [Guatemala, 1737-Mexico, 1945].

Leprestre de Vauban, Sebastien *A Manual of Siegecraft and Fortification* translated by George A. Rothrock [U. of Michigan, 1968].